AN UNTHINKABLE CRIME

Debbie Brisson pulled into the driveway of Terry Robertson's house, an attractive brick home in a shaded subdivision of Rock Hill, South Carolina. The two women had been friends for years.

Debbie parked in the driveway behind Terry's Cadillac, got out and rapped on the door in the carport. When no one answered, she walked around to the back door. The storm door was ajar; the glass in the wooden door shattered. Odd, Debbie thought, but turned the knob and stepped inside. It was dark as she made her way through the basement and up the stairs.

"Terry! Terry!" Her heart raced as the sound pierced the stillness.

At the top of the landing, she pushed open the door. Her eyes still adjusting to the light, she walked down the short hall past the bathroom, turned the corner and headed toward Terry's bedroom. As she rounded the corner, she stumbled over something on the floor.

Earl Robertson lay facedown, his skull smashed, blood everywhere. But where was Terry?

An investigator would later say that Debbie Brisson had somehow stumbled into a real-life horror movie.

BOOK YOUR PLACE ON OUR WEBSITE AND MAKE THE READING CONNECTION!

We've created a customized website just for our very special readers, where you can get the inside scoop on everything that's going on with Zebra, Pinnacle and Kensington books.

When you come online, you'll have the exciting opportunity to:

- View covers of upcoming books
- Read sample chapters
- Learn about our future publishing schedule (listed by publication month *and author*)
- Find out when your favorite authors will be visiting a city near you
- Search for and order backlist books from our online catalog
- Check out author bios and background information
- Send e-mail to your favorite authors
- Meet the Kensington staff online
- Join us in weekly chats with authors, readers and other guests
- Get writing guidelines
- AND MUCH MORE!

**Visit our website at
http://www.kensingtonbooks.com**

FAMILY BLOOD

LYN RIDDLE

PINNACLE BOOKS
Kensington Publishing Corp.
http://www.kensingtonbooks.com

For my family,
no one and nothing matters more.

ACKNOWLEDGMENTS

Special thanks to Meredith Moon for her cooperation. It was not easy for her to sit day after day in a prison visitation room and recount the murders of Earl and Terry Robertson.

To my agents, Frank Weimann and Karen Hass, my sincere appreciation.

To my editor, Michaela Hamilton, my gratitude for her patience.

To my family—my husband, Don, and our children, Josh, Lauren and Colin—my undying and unconditional love.

Lyn Riddle
Simpsonville, South Carolina
May 19, 2003

Part 1
The Murders

Chapter 1

In a bigger city, no one might have known what had happened in the Robertsons' brick ranch for many hours, perhaps even days. But as it was, Rock Hill, a town of 45,000 in north-central South Carolina, offered no such anonymity. An impromptu telephone tree emerged quickly as Earl Robertson became late for work and Terry Robertson did not pick up a coconut cake she had asked a friend to bake.

It unfolded well before nine o'clock in the morning on a brisk Carolina fall day.

Martha "Sissy" George made the first call. She had Terry's coconut cake. She called Linda Weaver, who had known Terry since Terry moved to Rock Hill as a young bride twenty-seven years earlier. Linda called Carolina Counseling, where Terry worked on occasion, and told Debbie Brisson, the office manager, that Terry had not picked up the cake. They all tried the Robertsons' number. They tried again and again. Every time, voice mail picked up on the first ring. They told themselves Terry was on the phone or had taken the phone off the hook. Still, something felt alarming.

It was November 25, 1997, two days before

Thanksgiving. The sun shone, yet the temperature wasn't expected to rise above the 40s.

Debbie Brisson tried to reassure herself as she drove toward Westminster Drive, a shady lane of attractive brick homes in a subdivision outside of Rock Hill, that perhaps Terry had just overslept.

Meanwhile, at Springs Industries, where Earl was the director of manufacturing, Margie Jordan's worries grew with every minute her boss was not in his office. Earl had scheduled an eight o'clock meeting. At forty-nine years of age, Earl was a creature of habit. He had worked at Springs for twenty-seven years and had never missed a day. The largest private employer in the area, Springs made textiles, bed and bath products mainly. Springmaid and Wamsutta were the company's chief brands. Earl's responsibility was to oversee all the administrative functions for manufacturing, including printing and long-range planning, a job that required organizational skill as well as the ability to solve problems and analyze and interpret data. People considered him brilliant. He was an engineer, a bit of a geek. Earl was the kind of man who arrived thirty minutes early for everything. One day mirrored another in his world, and he liked it that way. His secretary considered him a Southern gentleman to the core.

His wife, who was also forty-nine years old, was not at all structured. She was disorganized—so much so that her house was often a mess and even the most basic of household chores—cooking—was rarely done. But she was fun-loving, fun to be around. She had many friends, some of whom she talked with on the phone almost every day. Terry was the kind of woman who would pick up a knickknack at the store, select an appropriate card and leave the package on the porch of a friend just to say she was thinking of her.

Margie Jordan called the York County Sheriff's Office.

Greg Maggart, a patrol deputy in York County for seven years, took the call to check on the Robertsons. He drove his black-and-white cruiser to Westminster Drive and rang the bell at the front door. No answer. He walked around to the side of the house, into the carport, and knocked on the door. A small white dog barked loudly. Maggart looked inside through the large window in the door. It seemed a normal middle-income household. The wooden kitchen table was cluttered with groceries. The walls were painted a cheery yellow. He noted a Cadillac, more than just a few years old, parked in the carport, an aged Chevy van in the driveway. When no one came to the door, Maggart walked over to talk to a neighbor working in his yard.

"Have you seen the Robertsons today?" Maggart asked.

"If the red car's gone, he's gone," the neighbor responded. "He leaves for work before I get up and comes home after I go to bed."

Convinced all was well, Maggart radioed dispatch. He told the dispatcher the house seemed secure and advised he was clearing the scene. The response came back: call the original caller. Maggart drove about a mile to a gas station on the main road to a pay phone to call Margie Jordan.

"Earl Robertson has never missed a day of work," a frantic Jordan told the deputy. "He is the first here and the last to leave. He called a meeting and didn't show up. Something's wrong."

Maggart told her what he saw. Nothing.

"The son just got out of prison and moved back in there," she said in desperation.

For Maggart, that piece of information changed the entire picture. He headed back to Westminster Drive.

In the meantime, Debbie Brisson had pulled into the driveway of her friend's house. She had known Terry for almost two years. Terry had other friends she had known much longer, such as Linda Weaver, but she and Debbie had grown close in a short time. Terry helped Debbie deal with her loneliness when Debbie's daughter left for college. Debbie listened while Terry related the challenges of raising two sons, both now in their twenties. They talked on the phone every day.

Debbie parked in the driveway behind Terry's Cadillac. The van the Robertsons used for trips was in the driveway, and Earl's car was gone. Debbie rapped on the door in the carport. When no one answered, she walked around to the back door, into the backyard hidden from other homes by aged pine and oak trees. She thought Terry would better hear her knocking from there, since that door was beneath her bedroom.

The storm door was ajar; the glass in the wooden door shattered. Odd, Debbie thought, but turned the knob and stepped inside. It was dark as she made her way through the basement, which had full windows on the backyard side. It had been fashioned into a two-bedroom apartment with its own kitchen and bath for the Robertsons' sons.

Debbie called, "Terry! Terry!" The sound pierced the stillness like a thunderclap. Her heart raced, but she walked through the downstairs playroom—the room where Terry's boys entertained friends with billiards and music—and up the stairs.

At the top of the landing, she pushed open the door and, her eyes still adjusting from darkness to light, walked down the short hall past the bathroom, turned the corner and headed toward Terry's bedroom. As she rounded the corner, she stumbled over something on the floor.

Earl Robertson lay facedown, his skull smashed, blood everywhere.

All Debbie could think of was getting out. She didn't want to see what was in Terry's bedroom. And she didn't know whether she was alone in the house. She gingerly stepped around Earl, whose six-foot frame was clad only in white briefs, and fled away from Terry's bedroom, toward the front of the house, through the living room. She jerked on the double front doors, but they were secured with a dead bolt that locked with a key.

She turned and darted into the kitchen to go out through the carport. The kitchen door held fast; again, a keyed dead bolt barred her escape. She reached for the phone, which was off the hook. She quickly replaced it, then picked it up to call her office. Breathlessly, she told her boss, a family therapist, what she had seen. Call 911, he responded.

Just then, Deputy Maggart arrived. He saw Brisson through the window as she frantically jerked at the doorknob. She motioned that all the doors were locked from the inside.

He pointed her to a window on the back side of the house where the deck was and told her he would pull her through the window after she unlocked it. She dived through the window, screaming, "He's dead! He's dead! He's dead!"

An investigator would say later that Debbie Brisson had somehow stumbled into a real-life horror movie.

It was about 10:00 A.M.

Lieutenant Gary Rollins, who was the supervisor for York County Sheriff's Office uniform patrol unit, answered Maggart's call for backup. Maggart locked the sobbing Brisson inside his patrol car and the two deputies walked around the back to go in the same way Brisson had. They looked at the broken window in the door and walked inside. They checked each room downstairs, two bedrooms adorned with posters on the walls and discarded clothes on the floor—true signs of teenage boys in the house—a bathroom and a main living room, with an over-stuffed sectional sofa in a beige Indian print, a brick fireplace and a pool table. They found no one and headed upstairs.

A few steps beyond the top of the stairs, they found Earl Robertson beaten with a blunt object on the back and gouged in the head. Blood and brains oozed from his skull onto the light blue carpet and clung to the walls. Blood pooled around him. His back bore a strange mark, not a bruise but not a cut, either, about the size of a pipe, down the middle. His hands were tucked underneath his abdomen. Blood spatters marred the light blue walls and a nearby white door and its frame. Blood, as if sprayed from a misting bottle, splattered straight lines, dozens of them, on the ceiling. On the floor near his body lay a pair of blue jean shorts, a towel and a pair of Air Jordan basketball shoes, all bloodstained. A bottle of Tilex lay beside his left leg.

They saw a light on in a room at the back of the house. All other doors in the hallway were closed. Rollins told Maggart he would stay there and directed him to check the lit room. Maggart stepped over Earl Robertson and stealthily walked into the bedroom, his gun drawn. His heart beat wildly. As he lunged into the room, he saw a kitchen knife—its tip broken—on a bloody rose-colored sheet in the middle of a queen-size bed. Then he saw an arm, sticking up from a mass of linens.

Terry Robertson lay on her back between her bed and the wall. A blood-soaked flowered comforter had been pulled from the bed and lay on top of her, covering most of her body. The sheets showed the struggle she waged: deep clots of blood stained the fabric, but only on one side. The knife lay where she must have lain moments earlier. The slashes and stabbings on her plump frame were deep and numerous. Her throat was slit, from below her ear to under her chin. Another deep gash sliced open her face from behind her ear to her mouth. She wore a white nightgown with a print of tiny pink roses. A white desk phone, still bearing the number from the years the family lived in Fresno, California, sat atop a stack of catalogs, its base stained with small specks of blood. Her billfold, a pack of checks, a few small scraps of paper and a Blockbuster membership card—the contents of her black leather pocketbook—spilled onto the floor near her feet.

Maggart saw no need to check for a pulse. It was

clear she was dead. He repeated his arms-extended, gun-drawn check of each room as Rollins stood by Earl Robertson's body.

Convinced there was no life in the house, the deputies went out the same way they came in, closed the door and secured the scene.

Maggart, a native of nearby Fort Mill, came from a law enforcement family. His father was chief deputy of the very department he worked for. His uncle retired from the department as a lieutenant. Several cousins worked in law enforcement in other cities. He was used to the life. At thirty-six, he had worked other homicides. Yet, he had never seen one so brutal. He remembers it as the scariest time he's ever had. His whole body shook as he went room by room in a house that looked so much like everyone else's.

The amount of violence was beyond the imaginations of any of the investigators who worked the case. Later, an investigator would say, "That guy's head looked like a crushed tomato."

"Notify detectives," Rollins called to dispatch. "Two victims deceased."

Maggart and Rollins strung yellow crime-scene tape around the Robertson yard. Then with military precision, the work of investigators and the coroner and medical examiners and a forensic unit began.

The York County coroner would officially set the cause of death. It was required by law, but in this case the coroner's ruling would not tell anyone anything they didn't already know. No one could dispute this was homicide, and it was perfectly clear what killed them. Ralph Misle and Tim Hager, the homicide investigators for the county, were called to find out who did. Agents from the State Law Enforcement Division (SLED), which provides forensic investigations for all departments in South Carolina except the largest cities, were called as well.

Misle and Hager had worked together for a couple of years. Hager was the lieutenant in charge of the crimes-against-persons unit. York County had few murders, no more than ten a year, usually more like five, not enough to warrant a full-time homicide unit. Most of its work involved investigations of armed robbery and fraud. Hager considered Misle one of the best financial-transaction fraud investigators he'd ever seen.

Misle had been in South Carolina for eight years, a deputy for seven. A native of Queens, New York, he worked for the New York City Police Department for fifteen years. He retired in 1989, deciding on early retirement after a friend with the Federal Bureau of Investigation was shot and killed, ostensibly by the mob. Misle worried his work could make his wife a widow and his four-year-old daughter fatherless.

He went from the NYPD to a dry-cleaning business in Rock Hill, South Carolina. Retirement from law enforcement didn't last long, however. A year later, York County sheriff George Eaton, also an NYPD retiree, hired him as a narcotics investigator. Misle then moved to fraud and bank robbery investigations and worked homicide as needed.

Rock Hill was both a flourishing suburb of fast-growing Charlotte, North Carolina, and a staid college town, home to Winthrop University. Its only brush with national attention came years before when the Catawba Indian Nation won a $50 million settlement from the federal, state and local governments to end its claim to owning most of the town and the surrounding county.

Hager had grown up in Rock Hill. He never intended to be a cop. What he dreamed of was major-league baseball. A star catcher at Rock Hill High School, Hager spent three years playing college ball before he was drafted by the Texas Rangers. He played as a pitcher in the minor leagues, but ended his career when he became convinced that the magic moment when everything jelled to make his pitch perfect wasn't coming. As it was, he could throw hard, but he couldn't throw strikes. His three roommates ended up with satisfactory careers in the major leagues. He took a job as a deputy patrolman for York County in 1981, thinking he'd work long enough to figure out his true calling.

He had been around law enforcement during his youth. His grandfather was a policeman in Bessemer City, North Carolina. It seemed the thing to do. Here he was, now, sixteen years later and in charge of the crimes-against-persons unit for four years. The responsibility of figuring out who killed a prosperous and apparently well-liked couple in his hometown rested with him. He had taken an extended Thanksgiving holiday and was sitting in a deer stand near his home when his pager beamed the news of the double homicide. He changed clothes at home quickly and drove to Westminster Drive.

Investigators briefed Misle and Hager about what was inside the house. Misle didn't see the need to go in. People traipsing through crime scenes are investigators' enemies. Everyone who goes in and out brings something in and takes something with them, complicating the forensics and possibly altering the evidence. There was a notable case in nearby Greenville, South Carolina, where a wealthy matron was stabbed with a knife and screwdriver. Fingerprint experts found only one perfect print inside the house that belonged to someone other than a family member, heightening hopes that a tough case would be solved. It turned out to belong to an assistant prosecutor who had been watching the collection of evidence.

Misle and Hager began interviewing neighbors.

They quickly learned the Robertsons had two sons, James, known as Jimmy, and Earl junior, known as Chip. James, the oldest, had been living with his parents since Friday, four days earlier. He worked in the cafeteria at Winthrop. Chip was a student at the University of Pennsylvania's Wharton School of Business and lived on Forty-first Street in West Philadelphia.

A blue Honda Accord parked on the grass at the edge of the Robertsons' property was traced to Douglas Moon, a truck driver who lived in a condominium complex not far away, behind one of Rock Hill's too-numerous strip shopping centers. Someone would go to find Moon.

Wayne Langley, a neighbor across the street who was a friend of Hager's father, told Hager he saw Jimmy Robertson just before eight that morning. Langley had taken his daughter to work at a nearby day care and saw Jimmy and a woman he did not know putting something in the trunk of Earl's red car. It was actually the car Earl bought for Chip, but he had taken it back and was driving it himself.

Jimmy waved pleasantly, said Langley, who had

known the Robertson boys for years. When the Robertson boys were younger, Langley often saw the father outside tossing around a football or shooting hoops with them. Beth, Langley's daughter, was about the same age. Langley remembered that Jimmy came across the street to introduce himself when the family moved in.

Next-door neighbor William Wood told investigators Jimmy Robertson broke into his house about a year earlier and took his camcorder, television set, jewelry, checks and credit cards. He also stole his Toyota Celica. Robertson used the Sears card to buy six televisions, six VCRs, several radar detectors and a set of tires, some $3,800 in merchandise. A check was written to a florist for roses.

Wood initially thought Robertson was an OK kid. He talked politely and seemed clean-cut, but then he turned around and stole most everything of value that was in plain sight in Wood's house.

Later, Wood told a newspaper reporter for the *Rock Hill Herald,* "You think you know somebody, and you don't. We didn't see all of the stuff. Some of the other neighbors saw him as a troublesome kid all along."

Misle went back to the Moss Justice Center to work the phones and track any credit card use. He suspected credit cards had been stolen, since Terry Robertson's pocketbook had been dumped out and Earl's billfold was found open on the floor.

Jimmy Robertson, once a promising engineering student at Georgia Institute of Technology, was fast becoming the chief suspect. He had left a note amid a jug of detergent and other groceries on the table in the kitchen. "Mom and Dad Gone to get Chip in

his car—sorry but he needs me right now. Love,
Jim," it said.

Misle learned probation officers had been at the
house the day before and found marijuana. They
wrote him up for a parole violation, not only for the
pot but also for moving without permission. The
sheriff's office put out a BOLO (be on the lookout)
for the car, a red Mazda, and put Robertson's probation violation down as the reason.

They described Robertson as armed and dangerous.

Misle saw from a rap sheet Robertson was arrested in the theft at the neighbor's house and
pleaded guilty to two counts of grand larceny, sec-
ond-degree burglary, forgery and fraudulent use
of a credit card. A judge sentenced him to six years
in prison. At the time, he told investigators he sold
the merchandise to buy drugs. The roses went to
a girl. Drug possession charges were dismissed,
pending completion of a drug treatment program.

In his confession, he said he broke a latch on a
front window of the neighbor's house early one
Saturday morning and wore socks on his hands as
he methodically moved through the house, taking
whatever he thought he could sell. He went back
several times that day.

Robertson was sent to Lee Correctional Institution
in Bishopville, South Carolina, on September 3, 1996.
He was twenty-two, two months shy of twenty-three.
Corrections reports showed he had counseling at Lee,
took part in Narcotics Anonymous and completed a
stress and anger management course.

Robertson spent ten months in prison. He was

paroled the last day of July in 1997, barely four months earlier.

Investigators subpoenaed phone records and put a trace on the father's credit cards. They learned Jimmy Robertson had twice called his brother early that morning, once at 2:33, a thirty-four-minute call, and then again at 3:07, a three-minute call. He apparently hung up and called right back. Philadelphia Police Department was notified and campus police were dispatched to Chip Robertson's apartment. South Carolina authorities asked them to wait outside in the event Jimmy Robertson showed up.

Hager, meanwhile, spent the afternoon at the house. He went inside when the forensics team from the State Law Enforcement Division arrived from the state capital, Columbia, about ninety miles to the south.

Years later, he said, "I've never seen anything like it and I've been here twenty-two years. Nothing even comes close."

What was especially troubling was to see the amount of rage the killer obviously felt toward his victims. That indicated a clear emotional tie. Strangers do not inflict that sort of brutality. Hager knew even before the results of the autopsy came back some of the knife wounds on Terry Robertson's body had been inflicted after her heart had stopped beating. She was dead, yet the killer was still slashing.

Chapter 2

Douglas Moon had never met Jimmy Robertson. He didn't know his daughter, Meredith, was seeing him, either. All he knew was Robertson was a guy Meredith had worked with at Papa John's pizzeria. His daughter told him Robertson was a nice guy, that he waited until his coworkers were safely in their cars after closing before he'd leave.

In the early-morning hours on that Tuesday, he remembered it as sometime between 1:30 and 2:00, the ringing phone at the condominium he shared with his daughter woke him up. He and Meredith answered simultaneously.

"I got it; it's Erin," Meredith told her father.

He hung up, and as he was drifting back to sleep, Meredith came into his room and said she was going to Erin's house. Erin Savage and Meredith had been friends since they were in middle school. Meredith said Erin had hurt her finger and needed to go to the emergency room. She was going to take her.

"You need me to go with you?" he asked his daughter.

No, she could manage by herself, she said.

His daughter was still gone when he got up. As Moon dressed for his job at Rock Hill Printing and

Finishing, a subsidiary of Springs Industries, he heard a knock at the door. Two York County sheriff's deputies stood outside.

"Oh, my God, she's been in a wreck," he sputtered to the detectives as he opened the door.

"No, sir," one said. "It's much more serious than that."

The news that his daughter could somehow be caught up in the double murder of Robertson's parents hit him hard, like a "ton of bricks," he would say later. He was devastated. Not only couldn't he believe it, he didn't believe it. For more than an hour, he sat motionless, stunned, fearful for his only child. He didn't know where she was or whether she was even alive.

Meredith was a good girl. She had never gotten as much as a traffic ticket. Earlier in the year, she had graduated from Rock Hill's Northwestern High School, where she was in the Air Force Reserve Officers Training Corps in her junior and senior years. She worked regularly, mainly in restaurants, and had once harbored a dream of going to the University of Georgia to become a medical examiner. Something about forensic science interested her.

Meredith Moon was the kind of girl people usually described as having a pretty face. She was tall, to be sure, nearly six feet, but she was mostly just fat. In contemporary terms, she looked much like the rotund Gwyneth Paltrow in the movie *Shallow Hal.* Once a coworker greeted her with, "Hey, Kool-Aid," referring to the Kool-Aid drink pitcher. It was a sad reminder of all the harassment she took in school. Other students had called her "fatty" and told her she was as big as the moon, as if that were some clever play on words. She would walk down the hall in school to the same refrain: "Hey, fat girl." She had never had a serious boyfriend. Weight was a lifelong problem for her. When she was in fifth grade, she was taken by her mother to Weight Watchers. She weighed 187 pounds.

In November 1997, when the Robertsons were murdered, she weighed nearly three hundred.

"Most boys don't want to mess with a fat girl," her father, who was a large man himself, said some years later.

At the detectives' request, Moon called Erin Savage to see what she knew.

"The police are here," he told Erin.

Erin told him she had spent several hours with Meredith the night before, but not long after midnight, both girls were in their respective homes. She hadn't seen Meredith since. She told Moon she picked Meredith up at about 11:30 P.M., after Erin finished her shift at Outback Steakhouse, where she was a waitress. They went to Erin's apartment and played games on the computer and watched television. At about midnight, the phone rang. It was Robertson. He wanted them to come over. Erin wanted to go because she wanted Robertson to look at a pool cue she bought for her boyfriend. She wanted to know if it was a good one.

Erin drove her Chevrolet S-10 pickup over to the Robertsons' house. They parked in front and went around to the back door, which led into Jimmy Robertson's living room and bedroom. His friends thought of it as his bachelor apartment, a whole basement of the house transformed into his sanctuary.

He was cleaning up. He said family was coming

for Thanksgiving. Savage and Moon stayed for a short while, and then Erin drove Meredith home. Erin went home, too, put on her pajamas and settled in to watch television. At about 3:30 that morning, Jimmy Robertson called looking for Meredith, Erin said. She told him Meredith had gone home.

All she knew about Meredith's whereabouts was that Meredith called early that morning to say they were at a gas station and they were on their way to pick up Robertson's brother in Pennsylvania.

After the detectives left, Douglas Moon called his ex-wife, Patty Durand Moon, Meredith's mother. Patty lived in Duluth, Georgia, a northern suburb of Atlanta. They had maintained a good relationship in the six years since they divorced. It was a true no-fault divorce, they said. Their lives just didn't intersect. He worked as an over-the-road truck driver and she couldn't live with the separation. She needed companionship. Yet their friendship endured. They talked on the phone at least once a week.

"Meredith is missing," he told her, and explained what he knew. He realized then that what he knew was much less than what he didn't.

Chapter 3

At the Springs office in Lancaster, where Earl Robertson worked, employees learned about midmorning that he and his wife had been murdered. Some wept openly; others stood by speechless. Everyone felt stunned. Who could possibly have killed the man they knew as a kind and caring person, the one executive who always wanted to know how a change in the way the company did something would affect the people who had given so much of their lives to work there?

Miller Deaton, Earl's supervisor, had learned from Earl's secretary that he was late and that she had called the sheriff's office in York County. Now she was the one to come to him and tell him Earl was dead. Deaton was dumbfounded. He had recruited Robertson for the job five years before because of his analytical mind and his vast knowledge of the company.

He did not know him outside of work. He saw the Robertsons socially several times each year, and knew nothing of any trouble with their sons. Quite the contrary. Earl Robertson had proudly described Jimmy's acceptance to Georgia Institute of Technology, Earl's alma mater, and Chip's to

Penn. Robertson seemed to have a great deal of pride in his boys.

So when Deaton learned one of them was suspected in the deaths, he was shocked. "You don't know what you don't know" was how he described his reaction.

He and others at Springs couldn't help but wonder whether they missed something, something that could have averted what Deaton called a "true American tragedy."

Linda Hook was at home when her husband, Dr. George Hook, a golfing buddy of Earl's, called from his dentistry office.

"Are you sitting down?" he asked. "It's about Earl."

He told her the news. Linda ran out the front door and screamed at the top of her lungs. Even though she and Terry were not day-to-day friends, or even week-to-week friends, the pain was immeasurable. They had shared many confidences in the fifteen years or so their sons were in school together and the years they attended the same church.

She had had too many conversations with Terry about Jimmy's problems to be surprised that he was a suspect. She suspected Jimmy the moment she learned her friend was dead.

As morning passed into afternoon, the scene outside the Robertsons' house had turned into one of quiet chaos. A television truck toting a satellite dish rolled into the neighborhood, and reporters, print and broadcast alike, spread out interviewing neighbors. At one point, the narrow street became choked with cars from law enforcement, friends and reporters.

Patrolman Maggart stood guard in the driveway at the edge of the street, letting only certain law enforcement officers beyond the yellow crime-scene tape. He recorded each name as he let the officers pass.

The Reverend William T. Pender stood in the crowd. Tall and fit with curly brown hair, Pender had been the Robertsons' pastor for eight years. The Robertsons were in that 10 percent of members who do 90 percent of the work in a church, so Pender knew them and their boys well. His own children were younger than Chip and Jimmy Robertson, but Oakland Avenue Presbyterian was a church that cared for and knew the youth. Its youth program was one of the more active in town. Mission trips, youth retreats, the opportunity to serve the greater community, were readily available to the dozens of young church members and their friends.

No more than a couple of years earlier, Jimmy Robertson had taken Pender's offer to be part of the Sunday-after-Christmas youth service. Robertson was in his first year at Georgia Tech. It was an annual holiday rite for Pender. He took all the college students to lunch the Sunday before Christmas to ask if they'd play a role in the next Sunday service. Most often, the teens would agree to something simple, perhaps to offer the call to worship or the benediction. That year, Robertson and a few others agreed to do the sermon. Their subject was *Babette's Feast,* a film about a maid who spends her inheritance on a feast for the dour sisters who were her employers. The youth talked about how that idea figures into the experience of being a Christian.

Now, two years later, a parishioner had called to tell Pender something was going on at the Robertson house. They didn't know what but said it was "really bad." Pender was preparing to go to Montreat, North Carolina, one of three conference centers owned by the Presbyterian Church USA. His extended family was to spend Thanksgiving there together. His sister from Richmond, brother from Rock Hill and parents from Georgia all were expected to gather at the mountain retreat for the extended weekend.

Instead, he drove his car to the Robertson house, parked and walked toward the house. An officer told him the Robertsons were dead. People stood nearly speechless, looking quizzically at the brick house. Sheriff Bruce Bryant came, as did friends of the family. So did Tommy Pope, the man who would prosecute whoever was arrested for the crime. Pope, tall and angular with a shock of black hair, had become known far beyond Rock Hill and South Carolina for his prosecution of Susan Smith, the young mother who let her car slip into a Union, South Carolina, lake three years before with her young sons inside.

When Pope defeated the incumbent solicitor in the state's Sixteenth Circuit in 1992, the office had the worst backlog in the state. Slowly he had whittled it down and had handled several other murder cases besides Smith's. He had had few setbacks, except not securing a death penalty for Smith. When he ran for reelection, he won with 80 percent of the vote. A jovial, blackslapping lawyer, Pope was given to pronouncements such as "I see this job as a higher calling," "That which does not kill us makes us stronger" and "The devil came due." His presence at the Robertsons was noticed.

Pope didn't go inside the house but talked outside with detectives.

Pender stood there all afternoon. In his most honest moments, he'd acknowledge that part of the reason was because he was simply curious. But the main reason was he did not know what else to do. Certainly he had never experienced such a crisis in his church before, never seen such gruesome deaths of members. He worried about Chip and Jimmy, worried about how they would react when they heard the news. He wondered where they were. His life experience, his course work at Dartmouth, where he earned a bachelor's degree in economics, at Columbia Theological Seminary, where he earned a master's degree, and at Duke University, where he earned a doctorate, would have to be enough to help them and his congregation through this time.

Reporters asked him about the family. He said simply it was a tragic loss of a wonderful family. Asked to speculate about what happened, Pender refused. He assumed it was a break-in, some unknown assailant who came into the home and killed Earl and Terry.

Chapter 4

The detectives' trace through NationsBank on Earl Robertson's Visa card quickly paid off. Purchases on the card easily tracked Robertson's and Moon's route. The first hit was at the Peach Stand in Fort Mill, twelve miles north of Rock Hill. The gas station was one of the more unusual businesses in the area. It was owned by the Close family, who also owned Springs Industries and hundreds of acres of peach trees. The Peach Stand sold all manner of preserves and jellies, canned goods such as black-eyed pea salsa and apple cobbler, and their meats brought in people from miles around.

Early that morning, someone had used Earl Robertson's Visa card to buy gas and food, a $38.21 charge. A clerk told deputies a man and woman came in as if they were on a date, "happy as a lark." The couple said they were on their way to get the man's brother to take him on vacation. The clerk handed over the store's surveillance tape to the detectives. It showed Robertson and Moon standing at the cash register.

A calling card showed a call made from a rest stop on Interstate 85, north of Charlotte, the call to Erin Savage. That afternoon at about 2:00, the credit card was used again in Ladysmith, Virginia, to purchase gas, a charge of $13.68. Detectives were further convinced Robertson was headed for Philadelphia.

From Robertson's friends and roommate, the detectives learned Robertson had made some unseemly remarks about his father. He talked about putting cyanide in iced tea. Once he did it, he told his friends, but took the glasses away at the last minute. The friends did not know whether or not he was telling the truth. He talked about burning the house down. They knew Earl Robertson was a tightwad, who regularly berated his son for wasting money and for having jobs that could never earn what he considered to be a decent wage.

Earl Robertson earned a good salary, and through frugal living that, among other things, kept him driving an aged van, he had amassed a sizable estate. An avid golfer, Earl Robertson allowed himself one extravagance: the membership at Rock Hill Country Club. Misle learned Robertson might have been considering investing in a golf course. Jimmy Robertson's friends said he didn't like the idea that his father would spend the money that way because it would diminish his own inheritance.

Misle ran record checks on Moon and Robertson. Nothing came up for Moon, as her father predicted. Robertson not only had a criminal record, but also numerous traffic violations. His license had been issued in 1993. In the previous three years, he had been cited for speeding eight times, driving under suspension once, running a red light once, operating a vehicle in unsafe conditions once and failure to pay a fine five times. His license had been suspended and he had obtained a South Carolina identification card just a month earlier.

Detectives could only wait to see when and where Jimmy Robertson would show up.

At about eight o'clock that night, a red Mazda Protegé pulled up to Chip Robertson's apartment on Forty-first Street in Philadelphia. Four officers were there. They jerked Robertson and Moon out simultaneously—Moon by her hair—and they held the muzzles of their guns to the back of their necks.

Misle made plans to fly to Philadelphia.

Chapter 5

In Rock Hill, the quiet, unassuming Robertson family was on its way to infamy. Word of the brutal attack spread from a small circle at Springs to Oakland Avenue Presbyterian Church to Rock Hill Country Club, all the places that filled the lives of Terry and Earl Robertson. By nightfall, the evening news disseminated the news still further. By morning, both newspapers that circulated in the Rock Hill area had front-page stories on the murders.

The *Rock Hill Herald* headline blared: COUPLE FOUND DEAD AT HOME, while the larger *Charlotte Observer* said: COUPLE FOUND SLAIN IN HOME OFF INDIA HOOK.

In one thousand words, the *Herald* detailed the end of the Robertsons' lives. Sheriff Bryant told reporters there were no suspects, but authorities were looking for a red Mazda Protegé believed to be driven by the Robertsons' older son. The younger son, contacted in Pennsylvania, had been told of his parents' deaths.

"We really don't have a lot to report, to be honest with you," the newspaper quoted the sheriff as saying as he stood in front of the house.

The paper also had obtained Jimmy Robertson's criminal record and reported he had been incarcerated until earlier that summer. Coworkers described

Earl Robertson as a man of integrity—a steady, reliable guy.

"Earl was pretty focused and pretty dedicated getting the job done and not satisfied with less than excellent results. He was very demanding of himself," the paper quoted Bob Thompson, the Springs vice president of public affairs, as saying. "He was one of the most reliable people in the company. If you wanted a project ramrodded through, you gave it to Earl."

Terry Robertson was described as lovely and gregarious.

The *Observer* had fewer details of their lives and quoted neighbors about the shock they felt.

Friends who had known the Robertsons and each other for decades simply did not understand. They knew of Jimmy Robertson's troubles with the law and drugs, and some had begun to suspect he had killed his parents. But before that November day, they never could have imagined anything like what had transpired.

Linda and Bill Weaver. Ann and Dick Jordan. They had all been friends for nearly three decades, more than half their lives. The Weavers met Earl Robertson when he interviewed for a job at Springs shortly before he was to graduate from Georgia Institute of Technology. That summer, after he was hired by Springs and he and Terry married, the couples lived in the same apartment complex. They went to church together in those early days, too.

Linda felt like an older sister to Terry. The loss to her was immeasurable. And yet there were things to do. The Weavers and the Jordans would help Chip, who was twenty-two years old, plan the funerals. They thought of Earl's mother, the only surviving parent, in Newnan, Georgia. Reverend Pender arranged for a Presbyterian colleague to go with police to tell her about her son's death. In the meantime, Dick Jordan arranged for a plane to go to Newnan to pick her up. She had planned to be in Rock Hill for Thanksgiving. Her bags were packed when the group arrived at her door to say her only child was dead.

At eighty-four, Christine Robertson remained strong in body and mind, assured of her convictions. She told authorities that she knew something like this might happen. She had even confided to a friend that every time her son and his wife opened their door for Jimmy, they were taking their lives in their hands. Her son had told her on the phone just a few days before that Jimmy seemed all right then, but you never know what might set him off.

"The least little thing will make him crack," Mrs. Robertson told a reporter for the *Rock Hill Herald* on the day of her son and daughter-in-law's funeral. "And when he cracks, you never know what's going to happen." She told the reporter she had confided to a friend not that long before the murders: "He might go in there and kill them all."

Chip Robertson had been questioned for four hours in Philadelphia on Tuesday before his brother was arrested. Police called him and asked him to come into the station, which he did. On Wednesday, Misle and SLED agent Bobby Brown wanted to see him. They knew Chip Robertson had talked with his brother about three to four hours before his parents were murdered. Misle and Brown suspected Chip was somehow involved. He was the first one Misle wanted to see.

"We know your brother called you," Misle told him. "It was about the time he called Meredith."

"I don't know," Chip Robertson responded. "He didn't tell me anything."

No matter what Misle or Brown said, Chip Robertson's response was always the same: "I don't know. He didn't tell me anything." Chip Robertson did not waver. They let him go. It was the day before Thanksgiving. He went back to his apartment to find a care package with a honey-baked ham inside from his mother.

"They were the best in the world," Chip Robertson told a reporter for the *Charlotte Observer*. He left Philadelphia to return home to bury his parents.

With the help of the Weavers and Jordans, Chip selected Bass Funeral Home to handle the arrangements. The two-story white building was located on East Main Street, near downtown Rock Hill, and was a straight shot to the Robertsons' church, Oakland Avenue Presbyterian, a redbrick neo-Gothic edifice beside Winthrop University. Its mahogany pews, stained glass, gilded chandeliers and massive organ reflected the wealth of the thousand-member church, gave it an air of reverence. The congregation included college professors, doctors and corporate executives.

Chip and his grandmother met with Jay Denton, the manager of the funeral home. Chip seemed uncertain about what to do and was visibly upset, shaken. Denton gently led Robertson through the options. There was never a discussion of having an open casket, as is commonplace in the South. The deaths came under extraordinary circumstances and the Robertsons' bodies were horribly disfigured, especially their heads and faces. They could certainly be put back together, but it would require the work of an artist.

Visitation would be at the mortuary on Sunday night, the service at the church the next day. In the second-floor casket room, Chip selected matching pecan caskets with beige interiors, midpriced yet elegant. The funerals would ultimately cost about $16,000. Interment would be on Tuesday at Memory Hills City Cemetery, a historic graveyard in Milledgeville, Georgia, where Terry's parents were buried.

The November 27, Thanksgiving Day, edition of the *Charlotte Observer* carried the front-page headline: SON CHARGED WITH KILLING S.C. COUPLE. The story began with a simple declaration: "Earl and Terry Robertson tried to raise their sons right." Dad played ball; Mom was proud. Now they're dead and their oldest son was charged with their murder.

Sheriff Bryant told the *Rock Hill Herald:* "These kinds of cases never cease to amaze you how someone, especially to their parents, could be so cruel. Words can't describe it."

The next day, the *Observer* followed up with interviews with family friends. Friend Linda Weaver was quoted as saying, "Just a normal, middle-aged life." She talked about Earl playing basketball with the boys in the driveway and Terry being a Cub Scout den mother.

And all the friends were asking, "How can this be?" the article said.

Reverend Pender, preparing for what he would say at the funeral, couldn't help but remember seeing Terry and Earl dancing together at a Junior League dance. He knew that he would not be able to tie everything neatly in a sermon that would ease hurts, erase what had happened. Many years later, he said, "If you're playing the role of figuring it out, you're playing the wrong role. There's no good answer." He knew his job was to name the pain. From a theological standpoint, the best he could do was remind mourners that even Jesus, when He was resurrected, still bore His wounds. He was no longer in pain but the gashes remained.

The obituary notices, which ran that Saturday in the *Herald* and *Observer*, were short, without any hint of horrific death. The Weavers had helped write them. The announcements simply said the Robertsons had died at their home. Terry was a homemaker, a former English teacher, active in her church and the Junior Welfare League. She graduated from Agnes Scott College in Decatur, Georgia, in 1970. Her major was French, her minor art. Earl earned a bachelor's degree in textile engineering from Georgia Tech, and had been first in his class. He also had a master's degree in business administration from the University of South Carolina. He had worked for Springs Industries for twenty-seven years and was an avid golfer. They were members of the Rock Hill Country Club. The family asked that memorials be made to the Police Department Worthy Boys and Girls Club or to a church of one's choice.

Survivors were listed as their two sons, James Dejarnette Robertson and Earl L. "Chip" Robertson Jr., and Earl's mother.

On Sunday night at the funeral home, the line queued long before the seven o'clock start of visitation. In a small Southern town, the way funerals unfold is set with some rigidity. To be sure, there are family preferences: which funeral home is best, whether visitation should take place at home or at the mortuary. But visitation itself is a must-do, as necessary as taking casseroles, meat trays and chocolate rolls to the home. It's part of friends and family members paying their respects to those who have passed on.

By 7:00 P.M., the line flowed from the parlor, where the caskets stood before a bay window covered with curtains, down the winding hallway and out the back door, which led to the parking lot. Despite the rain, Springs workers, church members, longtime family friends, mingled in disbelief. They had so many questions, so few answers. How could such a thing happen in their community? To someone they knew? Someone they loved? What happened with Jimmy?

Monday morning, Chip Robertson and his grandmother filed into the ornate sanctuary of Oakland Avenue Presbyterian for the funeral. The mahogany pews were filled as the Reverend Pender mounted the elegant wood podium for his meditation.

"Our reactions over the past several days have run the gamut," he began, "beginning with 'It can't be' to 'It makes no sense' to 'I am so angry' to 'I am washed out and empty' to 'What will the future bring—with so many things that will never be completed—unfinished business?' This memorial service will not be a neat wrap-up of all we have experienced the past few days nor over the past years. We will continue to see dimly. We will continue to have anger in us. The emptiness will be like a hunger that is never fed. And the unfinished business will haunt us—the golf game that might have been, the graduation from college that still might be, the first grandchild, retirement, simply being together."

He said the group gathered there that day because each person was needy, yet each tried to deny it or bury it.

"We need each other and we need God," he said.

He said the need arose because each person was diminished by the deaths.

"More than a murder is here. There is theft as well. Time has been stolen away. We are all victims, some much more than others," he said.

He warned anger could consume them, could tear lives apart, and reminded them that the Lord said vengeance was not man's, but God's. He reminded the mourners that the pain could not be removed but could be shared.

"Together we are so much better than we are apart," he said. "We need each other. We need God because our resources are not enough."

He also reminded them that God shares the pain and hurt.

"We need God, who promises that one day, not today, and not next week, and not while any of us draws a breath, there will be no more tears, no more pain, no more death," he said. "We need a God who promises in Christ that there is a place prepared for us, that is now inhabited by Terry and Earl Robertson, where their wounds have been transformed, so they no longer limit, no longer hold them down.

"We need God and we need each other. We gather to remember the best that Terry and Earl gave to us and to set our lives anew on living before God and with each other, a faithful company. May the God who has given rest and peace to Terry and Earl strengthen us for the living of each new day."

Chip Robertson and his grandmother, Reverend

Pender, several of Terry's friends and a few other people drove to Milledgeville, Georgia, that night and stayed in a motel. Terry's friends talked about how angry they were at Jimmy Robertson. The next morning, a week after the murders, they gathered at Memory Hills City Cemetery, where the famed Southern author Flannery O'Connor is buried, and laid Terry and Earl Robertson to rest beside Terry's mother and father.

Chapter 6

In the week between the murders and the burial, law enforcement officers in Pennsylvania and South Carolina began building their case against Meredith Moon and Jimmy Robertson.

Ralph Misle of York County Sheriff's Office and Bobby Brown of the South Carolina State Law Enforcement Division were in Philadelphia the morning after Robertson and Moon were taken into custody. After Misle talked to Chip Robertson, he turned his attention to Moon, who had been handcuffed to a chair at the Philadelphia Police Department's "roundhouse" station all night and much of the day.

The night before, after her arrest, she asked officers as they arrived at the roundhouse where they were taking her. She was surprised when they responded "homicide." She thought to herself that she didn't do anything wrong. She didn't hurt anyone. She didn't even see the bodies. And then she wondered what Robertson would want her to say. She knew he wouldn't try to blame her. She believed he cared for her and only wanted what was best for her.

They put her in an interrogation room. Graffiti marred the wall. A policeman handcuffed her to a metal chair, where she sat for about three hours. She was allowed to go to the bathroom once, but was not given any food. As they took her sweater and shoes for analysis, they asked what was on her sweater.

"That looks like blood on your sweater," one officer said.

"I don't know," Moon responded.

A black woman in her late twenties, early thirties, whose looks and demeanor professed a tough life, was put in the room with Moon. Moon thought the woman looked like a gang member. She believed the police were trying to scare her and it was working.

Finally, about midnight, a Philadelphia police officer came in the room. She felt she had to say something. The officer told her he knew she was at the Robertson house. Her car was there.

Moon told him she was waiting in the car and did not know what Robertson was doing until afterward.

"I was scared," Moon said several years later. "That's the only thing I thought to say because I couldn't deny I was there."

After she gave a statement, they left her in the room. She fell asleep sitting up. Because she was handcuffed to the chair, she could not use her arm to cushion her head when she put it down on the metal table. When she wasn't sleeping, she was crying— silent, relentless tears.

When he walked into the sterile interrogation room in the Philadelphia Police Department, Misle had already learned a little about Moon and had formed an impression. She went to Northwestern High, had just graduated in fact, and was more of a follower than a leader. She had few friends. When she was booked the night before by the Philadelphia police, she weighed 292 pounds. She stood nearly six feet tall. Sadly, she became one of the girls teens so enjoy terrorizing with mimicry and sarcasm. Misle had met her father, who seemed like such a straight-up guy, soft spoken, looked a little like the actor Ernest Borgnine.

Misle also knew she wasn't a tough girl like so many of the girls he saw. The troubled girls. He called them "hard-asses." She was quiet and probably could be coaxed into telling what happened. After nearly twenty-five years as a policeman, he had a sixth sense about who would talk and who wouldn't. People in custody adopt one of three attitudes. They'll hem and haw but won't invoke the right to have an attorney present. Or they can't wait to talk, knowing the first to tell what happened usually gets the best deal. And then there are the folks who simply tell cops to go straight to hell.

He introduced himself politely and sat down across from her at the metal table. He read her the Miranda right to counsel. She was sitting in a straight-back chair, her thighs spilling over the sides. She agreed to talk. Misle brightened. He explained what they knew about her trip north with Robertson. He didn't want to lie to her outright, even though the U.S. Supreme Court had ruled law enforcement could use subterfuge in interrogation.

He pulled out a legal pad and said, "It's in your best interest to cooperate. I need for you to tell me what happened."

He told her she could remain silent and stay in jail or she could talk and go home. She looked scared, nervous, but was composed.

"I know you're involved, Meredith," he said. "You

left your car there. You were seen leaving the crime scene. We have a video from the Peach Stand that showed you in there."

He questioned her about her relationship with Robertson. She never said they were a couple, yet everybody assumed he was her boyfriend. She didn't precisely know what their relationship was. They didn't actually date but were together most of the time. He was the first boy who seemed to care for her.

Meredith said she had spoken to her friend Erin Savage about threats Jimmy Robertson had made against his parents. But they chose to disregard them. He was mad at his father more so than his mother, she told Misle, but Moon never took him seriously.

Misle let her talk. His method of interrogation was such that he didn't want the suspect to go right into details of the crime. He wanted to know how she got into the situation.

Finally she began her second version of events. She told her father she had to leave, that Erin had been hurt and she needed her. But the truth was Jimmy Robertson called and said to come over. He called around 3:30 A.M., then again about 5:00 A.M., when he called for the last time.

"We're leaving for Philadelphia," he told her on the phone.

Meredith pulled on brown corduroy pants and a brown sweater. She stopped at the Circle K convenience store on the way to the Robertsons' for Marlboro Menthol Lights. She parked her car facing the wrong way at the edge of the Robertsons' property. She went in through the downstairs door into the apartment that the Robertsons had fashioned for their sons. They sat down on the couch in the family room. Robertson crushed some Ritalin and they snorted it. Later they did more, probably ten lines in all.

"I'm going to do it," he declared. "I'm going to kill my parents."

He had talked like that before, Moon told Misle. Probably had been talking about it for a year. He told her his parents were worth a couple of million.

He explained his plan. When his father got in the shower, he'd kill his mother and then his father when he came into the hall. Earl Robertson was a creature of habit. His alarm rang at the same time every day. He showered and left the house, all the same, day after day. Jimmy Robertson was waiting to hear the alarm clock, and when he heard his father in the shower, he grabbed a metal baseball bat, a twenty-five-ounce Easton with a black grip, one he and his brother had used for playing ball.

Meredith said Robertson walked up the stairs. Meredith stayed downstairs, she said. She heard a struggle. And then Terry Robertson's screams. She cried out for her husband. She pleaded, "No, Jimmy."

The father was in the shower down the hall. He used it regularly because he didn't want to wake his wife. He could not hear her cries.

Moon said she sat downstairs, holding her hands to her ears. She rocked back and forth. After about a minute, she went outside on the downstairs porch and smoked a cigarette. The family's rabbit in a cage was running around in circles.

She went back inside and sat on the couch.

Soon Robertson called from upstairs.

"Meredith," he said in a loud whisper.

She walked up the steps and saw him at the end of the hallway.

"Go get me a knife from the kitchen," he said.

She tried to go out the garage door, but it was secured with a dead bolt. She said she just got a knife and gave it to him, then walked back down the stairs and sat on the sofa in Robertson's bedroom. The shower was still running.

When it stopped a few minutes later, she heard a thumping noise like a hand beating a pillow. It went on for a minute or so.

Then Robertson came back downstairs. Blood covered him. The picture of himself that was ironed onto his T-shirt couldn't be made out plainly.

Meredith said she went into the living room and he followed, but then he heard a noise upstairs. Robertson went back up to investigate.

When he came back down, he took off his clothes in the hallway and got in the shower. Fives minutes later, he was out of the bathroom and stuffing his bloody clothes into a trash bag. He put the bat, a hammer and a bottle of some sort of liquid that helps people beat drug tests into the bag as well. Moon helped him clean up the blood traces in the bathroom.

It was 7:45 A.M.

As they walked out the back door, Moon said, Robertson picked up a rake and broke a pane of glass in the storm door to make it look like a robbery. They drove out on South Carolina Highway 21, she said, and stopped at the Peach Stand for cigarettes, snacks and Band-Aids. Robertson cut his finger when he broke the window.

She detailed the other stops along the way. They

stopped in Virginia and Robertson called his house. He told Moon something was wrong. The phone rang and then voice mail picked up. It should have gone straight to voice mail, he said, because he had left a phone off the hook upstairs in the den.

Moon said when they stopped at a gas station and rest stop to use the bathroom, Robertson threw out the trash bag.

Misle stopped her and asked to be excused for a moment. He asked Brown to stay with her. Misle called his office.

"Call the Maryland Police Department right away," he said to his colleague Dean Schilling. He gave the location of the gas station and asked that they check the Dumpster.

Misle wrote out her statement and she signed it. He explained the extradition process and told her she would be taken to a facility until they could get a hearing in court.

He shook her hand and left. Moon was taken to jail. It was Thanksgiving. She ate the cheese sandwich the jailers gave her.

Misle went to talk to Robertson. James D. Robertson had always held his own counsel and relished a good game of cat and mouse. In his mind, he was always the cat. Misle saw that quickly. Robertson sauntered into the interrogation room and sat comfortably in an office chair. Misle read him his rights. Robertson said he understood. He looked more like a college preppy than a patricidal and matricidal killer.

"Here's what I know," Misle said. "Meredith's giving the whole thing up."

Robertson looked at him vacuously. No reaction.

"The Maryland State Police recovered a bunch of stuff from the Dumpster. Bat, knife, clothes. They're all full of blood."

Nothing.

He agreed to answer questions but said he'd answer only those he wanted to answer.

He told Misle where he lived, his parents' names. Then he said he didn't know what was in the bag that had been recovered in Maryland. Meredith told him to get it out of the trunk. He didn't even know how it got in the trunk in the first place.

He was without emotion. Yet this was the same fellow, Misle felt sure, who was so full of rage, the imprint of a metal bat was apparent on his dead father's back.

Cool and collected, Robertson said to Misle: "Only two people know what happened in that house—Meredith and me—the truth will come out at the right time."

The next day, bail was denied for both Robertson and Moon. When Moon was taken back to her cell, the officer asked if she wanted to make a phone call. They'd offered three or four times before and, as with those times, she said no. She felt she wasn't stable enough to call anybody.

Finally on Friday, she called her father. For Douglas Moon, the truth was almost more than he could bear. He had spent much of the previous two days sitting alone in his condominium, worrying about his daughter. He fully believed she was innocent, taken against her will, possibly a hostage, possibly dead or headed for it. When York County deputies told him she was in custody, it seemed like good news. He had called police stations in the Philadelphia area, trying to find out where she was and if she was all right. He had already been to the York County Sheriff's Office.

One of Meredith's half brothers—Moon's stepson—arrived from Georgia to be with him. His ex-wife had two sons from a previous marriage and they doted on their sister. Finally, at about nine o'clock, she called.

She was crying, near hysterics.

"Daddy, I didn't do it. Daddy, I didn't do it."

He was crying, too, and asking her to explain.

"Daddy, I am so sorry. Daddy, I'm sorry" was all she could say.

Douglas Moon tried to get some information from her, but she was crying so hard, she could barely talk. Five minutes to the second, the phone cut off. And Douglas Moon was left wondering.

Meredith felt only guilt. The telling of what she had heard offered no relief. She felt guilty for being there and for allowing it to happen. She especially felt guilty for not doing anything about it. She had never met Earl or Terry Robertson and knew precious little about Jimmy Robertson. She had known him for so little time. In fact, there were many things she knew nothing of, things that would loom large in the days to come. There were things that friends of the Robertsons didn't know. There were secrets inside the house at Westminster Drive, Rock Hill, South Carolina.

Secrets.

Part 2
The Family

Chapter 7

The sound of George Harrison singing "Here Comes the Sun" resounded through the dormitory at Agnes Scott College, where Terry Dejarnette was in her senior year. The summer before, four hundred thousand young people spilled across a farmer's field near Woodstock, New York, for a concert billed as three days of peace and music. Charles Manson engineered the slaughter of nine people in California. And Neil Armstrong walked on the moon. Yet, for blond-haired, perpetually smiling Terry Dejarnette, all served as, at most, a backdrop for a serene life on a campus of oaks and maples and aged redbrick buildings of the all-girls college in Decatur, Georgia, a suburb of Atlanta.

She had the look of most of her generation—long, straight hair, parted on the side. Her wide and easy smile captured the oxymoronic 1960s: innocence mixed with the possibility of wildness. At Agnes Scott, she chose French for her major, art her minor.

In those waning days of the turbulent decade of the 1960s, after the assassinations of Robert Kennedy and, closer to home, Atlanta resident Martin Luther King Jr., the riots at the Democratic Party convention and upsurge of drug use and the so-called free love, Agnes Scott remained ensconced in another time.

"It was very protective of us," remembered Sally Skardon, who lived in Hopkins Hall with Terry their freshman year. There were rules about what time to be home and signing out and an absolute ban on going into a man's apartment.

Regularly Terry took friends with her to her parents' home in Milledgeville, Georgia, which served as the state capital until the government center moved to Atlanta, one hundred miles to the northwest. Odd, considering the challenges that would consume Terry's later years, Milledgeville once was the home of the nation's largest insane asylum.

Ann Marquess or Beth Huminey or Sally Skardon or any combination of her friends made the ninety-minute trip with Terry to the Dejarnettes' modest but elegantly appointed house on Pine Valley Road. Terry's father, James Terry Dejarnette, a retired colonel, worked at the Youth Detention Center. Her mother, Dorothy, eleven years younger than her husband, sought her place in society.

Dorothy Dejarnette considered it "barbaric" to eat dinner before five o'clock in the evening. Highballs became a ritual. Bridge became a passion. She was particular about who won invitations to her many-times-a-week bridge games in her modern-style home in one of the first subdivisions to be built outside downtown Milledgeville.

"Dorothy had a streak as wide as a foot for social position," said one woman whose family dates back five generations in Milledgeville. "She did everything known to man to maintain ties with people who had social position."

It was not lost on Terry's friends that the statuesque Mrs. Dejarnette missed the order and prestige of being a colonel's wife. Her immaculate house, filled with books and antiques, reflected her need for organization. It was certainly not the way Terry lived at college. Disarray suited her best, a habit that would in many ways haunt her all of her adult life. She looked different from her mother, too. Where her mother had an almost modellike bearing, the daughter was short and small-boned.

The Dejarnettes' lives in the military swirled with adventure. They lived in a twenty-one-room house in France during one of the colonel's postings. Other stints took the family to Governor's Island in New York, Japan and Fort Sill, Oklahoma. While her mother relished the moves, the daughter's happy, outward demeanor masked her true feelings. She yearned to belong, to have roots, and she lacked self-confidence. When elementary-school teachers called on her to read, she would burst out crying. The frequent moves made Terry desperate for friends, and she felt she would do anything to keep them. The family moved to Atlanta as Terry was starting high school and she was sent to public school, an adjustment after being overseas and in private schools.

Painting served as an outlet for her, yet her first year in high school proved difficult. Her parents thought she might be suicidal and sent her to a psychiatrist. Yet her college friends saw someone very different. They remember a generous and open young woman, who would turn over her clothes to friends without a thought if they simply admired them. Terry liked activity, even chaos, noise. Her roommate for her first two years in college, Ann Marquess, was regularly driven out of the dorm room and into a study room by Terry's music.

Terry was not a disciplined student. She'd rather listen to people than complete assignments.

Her father, by contrast, was a quiet man who was thirty-nine when Terry, his only child, was born. His wife was twenty-eight.

Terry Dejarnette did not wait as long as they to find love. She was twenty-one when she met Earl Robertson at a fraternity party. Earl Robertson was first in his class at Georgia Institute of Technology in Atlanta, where he was studying textile engineering.

They could not have been more different. Terry seemed the life of the party; Earl was the shy, smart engineering student.

What Earl Robertson lacked in personality, he had in self-confidence. He was an orderly man, who knew what he wanted and how to get it. An Eagle Scout with close-cropped hair, and at twenty-one with a hairline already receding, he looked out of place with the free-love generation. It was apparent that hippies had not found their way to Georgia Tech, one of the South's finest private colleges, known especially for its engineering program.

He was reared in Newnan, Georgia, one hundred miles to the west of Milledgeville, in a modest house on what was known as "mill hill." Every textile town had a mill hill, a collection of shotgun houses owned by the mill owner. In previous generations when textile mills were the center of commerce in many a Southern town, mill owners typically rented the houses to workers, who also bought most of their food and other provisions from the store he owned as well. By the time Earl came along, textile companies had largely gotten out of mercantile and real estate and sold off the shotgun houses to the lower-middle-income residents of the town.

Earl Robertson proposed to Terry on Valentine's Day in 1970 after only a few months of dating. He had a plan for his life. He had interviewed at Springs Mills, Incorporated, which would become Springs Industries in 1982. The corporate headquarters was in Fort Mill, South Carolina, a small town twenty miles south of Charlotte, North Carolina. He would start a job there in the summer. He and Terry would marry in August after they both graduated from college.

Terry's parents considered Earl a good catch and thought Terry lucky to get someone like him. Terry thought it was perhaps the first thing she had ever done to please her parents, to make them proud of her. He offered stability and was a man with a future, a planner like her father. Terry felt closer to her father than her mother. Later in life, she described their bond as being as if they shared a special language, a way of communicating that no one outside could understand. She was proud he would walk her down the aisle.

For the daytime wedding, Terry selected the most formal attire. She wore a white gown, square neck trimmed in lace with illusion sleeves. Her veil was elbow length with a lace cap. She had let her golden hair grow longer since her graduation. It was a few inches past her shoulders and was curled at the ends.

Earl and his groomsmen wore traditional cut-aways, tailcoat-length dark gray coats, striped pants, wing collar shirts, pearl gray vests and ascot ties.

Nine bridesmaids dressed in green satin gowns and green illusion veils attended the couple. The historic First Presbyterian Church of Milledgeville shone with a glowing candelabrum at the altar and white flowers. The three sets of pews overflowed with friends and family members.

Terry walked down one aisle on the arm of her father as she entered the church, and after a simple Presbyterian service, she walked up the other aisle with her new husband. She beamed. He smiled shyly. It was a new beginning, a day when everything seemed possible.

Chapter 8

Earl helped Terry pack up her belongings for their move to Fort Mill, South Carolina. They had rented an apartment—where Earl had been living since starting his job a few months earlier. It was located in an apartment complex that was also home to other Springs professionals.

Earl's boss, Bill Weaver, and his wife, Linda, lived there. The couples passed their days off cooking on the grill and hashing out the issues of the day on the back porch of one or the other's apartment. Their bond deepened, especially that of Terry and Linda.

Both couples moved into houses in Fort Mill and their friendship grew. They spent holidays together and attended Unity Presbyterian Church.

Linda was the first to get pregnant. Terry followed two years later. A college friend who saw Terry shortly before she was to give birth to her first child remembered the excitement Terry felt at the prospect of a child, a family, someone to love unconditionally and someone who would return the feeling in kind. She wanted to provide what she didn't have growing up—stability, support, security, unconditional love. Terry showed the same sort of self-deprecating humor she had as a collegian. She told her friend she was getting so big, she'd soon need a shopping cart to get around.

On November 17, 1973, Terry and Earl's first child was born. It was Terry's mother's fifty-third birthday. They named their son James Dejarnette Robertson, in honor of Terry's father, the colonel. Two years later, they added another son, Earl junior, whom they dubbed Chip.

While Terry felt great joy in the births of her children, just as so many mothers before her, she felt tremendous anxiety about whether she would be able to be the mother they needed. Her mother added to her fears with regular criticism. At times, Terry believed she did not even know how to hold her son properly. She seemed to listen more to her parents than to her husband about how to raise the children. But it wasn't just failing as a mother that bothered Terry. She also felt she did not measure up as a daughter. She remembered as a child writing a note to her mother that said, "I know you will have a good day today. I am going to be so-so good."

But even as she felt inadequate and harbored negative feelings toward her mother, she was protective of her and wanted to please her. Terry Robertson was a woman who wanted to please everyone, who always put herself last. Her needs were second to those of her husband and her parents. Having sons simply caused her to put her needs behind yet another layer.

Earl, meanwhile, was working the corporate ladder. He started as a young engineer in the facilities-planning department, where he studied the future needs of the plants and decided which equipment to invest in. Soon his bosses were seeing the same eagerness and work ethic in him that Robertson's professors had seen.

In the late 1970s, Springs bought Seabrook, a frozen-foods company, based in Fresno, California. Earl was sent out as the third-ranking executive. Terry enjoyed those years with her husband and young sons. It helped moving away from her family and from Earl's mother. She felt her mother regularly stood in judgment of her, and Earl's mother offered no help at all.

Springs then sent Earl Robertson to Grand Rapids, Michigan. They bought a house on Boston Street in a pleasant subdivision south of downtown, not far from Metropolitan Hospital. Terry experienced some of the same feelings she had as a child, moving here and there. She did not like it and wondered about the effect on her boys. She worried that they did not fit in or felt out of step with their peers. She worried about the kind of men they would grow up to be.

She started to have feelings that she had "bad kids." Jimmy was in the early years of elementary school, a time of change, when someone outside the parents have a say in the development of the child. It can be unsettling for some that suddenly an outsider has a role in a child's life and by extension in the life of the parent. Teachers can't help but judge the kind of parenting that has gone on in a home. They learn intimate details of the lives of children and also their parents. Smart teachers have been known to tell parents: "I won't believe everything your child says about you, if you don't believe everything he says about me."

That was a concept Terry Robertson did not grasp.

She did not like the intercessions of teachers and, in turn, reacted like a mother tiger protecting her sons when she believed they were being misjudged, which was anytime someone criticized something they did. She might have negative feelings about her sons, but woe to anyone outside her immediate family who expressed anything other than praise.

Earl Robertson did not have time for her fears as he worked to move up the corporate chain.

They both kept in regular contact with their friends in Fort Mill, South Carolina. Linda Weaver and Terry talked regularly on the phone. Bill visited on business trips.

When Earl was transferred back to South Carolina about four years later, the Robertsons renewed their friendship with the Weavers and other couples. The Robertsons bought the house on Westminster. It was situated on a two-acre wooded lot, one of the largest in the subdivision. There were three bedrooms upstairs, a kitchen, den, living room and dining room, plus a full basement, where they could add rooms when their sons grew older. It was 1983; Jimmy Robertson was in the later years of elementary school, preparing to enter the perilous middle-school age.

Terry had a regular weekly lunch date with Linda Weaver. The Robertsons and the Weavers drove to Atlanta for Georgia Tech football games, celebrated birthdays, attended NASCAR races. Terry regularly attended Fort Mill High School's marching band competitions to support the Weavers' two children, who considered Terry an aunt.

Terry helped at the Junior Welfare League, a charitable and social services organization started in 1938. Earl and Terry were regulars at high-school basketball games and at Oakland Avenue Presbyterian Church, a stately church next door to Winthrop University. They were members of the Rock Hill Country Club, where Earl played golf, which was his passion.

Terry was president of the PTA and worked feverishly to raise money for the school. Sometimes she'd have dozens of projects going at a time. Most presidents before her had one major fund-raiser a year; she had seven. Sometimes she'd stay up all night planning PTA events. It mattered what people thought. She was going to be the best. She was going to please those around her.

The Weavers and the Robertsons spent Christmas together for years, usually at the Robertsons'. But then as Jimmy grew into his teens, the get-togethers became less frequent. The gatherings were difficult. Jimmy acted out. The Weaver children, one two years older than Jimmy, the other a year younger, did not enjoy being with him. The children, once young playmates, grew apart as they grew older.

In school, Jimmy Robertson was considered a weird kid. He was slightly built, even puny. What others didn't know was that he wet his bed until he was twelve years old. Students teased him because of his size and his awkwardness. He was never part of the in-group. Even in the Oakland Avenue Presbyterian Church youth group, he was something of an outcast. But he did play church basketball and took part in Boy Scouts with an idea of one day earning his Eagle rank, the highest in the Scouts and one that only 4 percent of Scouts ever attain, as his father had before him.

The more Jimmy Robertson drifted, the more his mother felt sorry for him. She could relate to how he was feeling. She knew what it was like to feel as if you don't belong. Once when he got in trouble for giving another child an answer on a test at Catawba Christian School, he was punished by having to clean bathrooms. His mother went to school in protest. The teacher Mike Faulkner remembered telling Terry Robertson that her son was troubled. He believed there was either a grave or a prison cell awaiting him. Terry said angrily, "There is nothing wrong with my son."

She cleaned the bathrooms herself.

Earl Robertson made it a priority to help his son earn his Eagle badge. He worked alongside fourteen-year-old Jimmy to complete his community service project. It was a high achievement and a point of immense pride for Earl Robertson. Another longtime Scout, whom Jimmy had known since elementary school and whose mother was a friend of his mother, had lost interest and ended up two badges short.

Terry Robertson knew it was Jimmy's behavior that had ended the Christmas tradition with the Weavers. Somewhere along the line, they lost Jimmy. Or he lost himself. His parents suspected he was using drugs, abusing alcohol. Yet they bailed him out time after time.

Terry Robertson's life was upended in 1988 when her father died of cancer. He was 79. She became racked with guilt that she was not there to care for him. She was not even there when he died. She felt she had abandoned him. Two years later, a week before her seventieth birthday, Dorothy Dejarnette,

Terry's mother, died as well. Terry's feelings of being a bad daughter grew stronger as her son Jimmy, her father's namesake, grew more and more out of control.

Still, Jimmy Robertson had major successes. He was accepted for the four-week program at the Governor's School for Science and Math at the College of Charleston. A prestigious program, the Governor's School accepts two hundred rising-star seniors each year.

Also in his junior year at Northwestern High, Jimmy Robertson applied for a scholarship that would give him a year of study in Germany. He competed against dozens of students in the area, including a son of one of his mother's good friends, the same fellow who had not earned the Eagle badge. Through each step, Jimmy Robertson excelled as others dropped out or failed. Résumés, essays, interviews. In the end, Robertson won, besting his high-achieving friend.

The time in Germany was one of unbridled freedom for the impressionable and immature teen. His problems grew worse with the dangerous mix of available beer and no real limits. Later, he remembered the time as the best eleven months of his life. His parents sent money—$1,000 a month—and he was free to travel and drink. Jägermeister, a potent liqueur best drunk extremely cold, was a particular favorite.

His mother wrote him every day and called frequently. When the telephone bill grew so large that Earl complained and told Terry to cut down, she drove to a pay phone and dropped quarters and dimes into the device just so she could hear her eldest son's voice. She was miserable without him.

He graduated from Northwestern High School in 1992.

In the fall, Jimmy Robertson enrolled in Georgia Institute of Technology, his father's alma mater. It was the setting where Earl Robertson came into his own and he hoped his eldest son would have a similar experience. Jimmy Robertson signed up for a full load—chemistry, economics, calculus, psychology, literature and language.

But the younger Robertson was not a clone of his father. In fact, his father sometimes wondered whether he was actually blood kin. Robertson made D's in chemistry, economics and calculus and a C in literature and language. He made an A in psychology. His grade point average was 1.50 and he was placed on academic probation.

His son's dismal college performance haunted Earl Robertson, who graduated first in his class. He felt humiliated before his former professors. His dreams for his son evaporated and Earl Robertson grew angry.

The next quarter was little better, except Jimmy Robertson managed B's in calculus and history. By spring, he had withdrawn from some classes, but even with the lighter load, he still earned C's and D's. He showed no improvement his sophomore year. By fall 1994, Robertson failed all of his classes except bowling, in which he made a D. His final GPA was 1.31.

Besides drinking and using drugs, he was gambling, sometimes losing a $1,000 on video poker in one sitting. He took his parents' checks and made them out for hundreds of dollars and forged his father's signature. He was getting ticket after ticket from the police: speeding, improper lane change, running a red light.

His parents tried to help. Sometimes, their friends

thought, their help seemed extreme and to his detriment. Financially, emotionally, they were there. They felt it was a parent's duty. It was part of loving their child. People told them they needed to practice something called "tough love," let the child stand on his own, for better or worse. Keeping him from hitting the bottom only kept him from getting better, friends told the Robertsons. Earl could do it, but Terry could not. And that difference caused a rift in their marriage.

Chapter 9

Douglas Moon and Patricia Durand met in 1971 when his brother married her sister. Patty was the maid of honor and Douglas was an usher. They were living in Monroe, Georgia, a town of about ten thousand people in the Alcovy River Basin, due east of Atlanta. It was a spot on the map for Atlanta-area football fans making the fall Saturday pilgrimage to see the Bulldogs of the University of Georgia play in Athens.

Three years after the siblings' wedding, Douglas was talking to his sister-in-law and casually asked, "Do you think Patty might like to go out to eat?"

"Ask her," came the reply. He did and she said yes. She had been married before and was raising two sons on her own, working as a licensed practical nurse. He had served in the navy until August 1967 and then signed on the next month as a truck driver for Ryder Truck Rental. Douglas's father worked for Ryder as did his brother. Douglas and Patty dated for a year and a half before they married on June 21, 1975, at Walker Baptist Church before an overflowing crowd of family and their friends from work. Douglas wore a tuxedo, Patty a pale yellow dress. She had a fever of 102.5 and one of the worst colds she'd ever had.

But they went ahead with the ceremony and the reception in the activities building at the church and then drove to St. Augustine for their honeymoon. It was raining when they checked into the Quality Inn on the beach and raining when they checked out two days later. On their way home, when they hit Jacksonville a few miles north, the sun came out.

It was an inauspicious beginning.

They bought a three-bedroom brick ranch and Douglas set out to plant some trees. He ended up with twenty-three oak trees in the back and fifteen in the front. They were beautiful in the summer and provided welcome shade in the semitropics of summertime Georgia. But in the fall, the leaves on the ground were a nightmare.

Almost four years after their wedding, Douglas and Patty had their first child, a girl, whom they named Meredith. Patty's sons, Andy, twelve, and Kenneth, ten, fussed over their baby sister. President Jimmy Carter, a fellow Georgian, was in the third year of his term, and just a week before Meredith was born, one of two reactors at Three Mile Island, near Harrisburg, Pennsylvania, lost its coolant, causing a partial meltdown of the uranium core. Some radioactive water and gases were released into the air. That year, Mother Teresa won the Nobel Peace Prize and *The Deer Hunter* was best picture.

Life moved on seamlessly for the Moons. Douglas continued his over-the-road driving; Patty stayed behind working and raising the children. Meredith was four years old when she picked up her first book and learned to read. It became a lifelong passion. She loved losing herself in the stories of Babar, the orphaned elephant raised by an old lady, and the Berenstain Bears, a wacky ursine family. As she grew, she read the Ramona Forever series and the Babysitters Club books.

She loved to read on the front porch or anywhere outside.

Her parents gave her most any material thing she wanted: a Big Wheel, a new bike. Attention was heaped on her from her parents and brothers. Her father was often gone, driving big rigs across the country. He liked to think he made up for his absence by bringing his daughter a present from every trip: a T-shirt, a Barbie, there was always a surprise.

She played T-ball, but she was never particularly athletic. As she grew older, she also grew fatter. However, luckily, she had not completely felt the sting of youthful jabs. She still maintained a sunny disposition.

One day when she was in fifth grade, Meredith wondered why there was not a holiday to celebrate neighbors. She wrote a letter to the mayor of Monroe and suggested one. He thought it a grand idea. Meredith, dressed in a denim jumper, rode her bicycle up to City Hall for the mayor's proclamation. The mayor gave her a plaque emblazoned with NEIGHBORS DAY and a big picnic unfolded on the town square.

The next year, the family went to Orlando to see her brother Kenneth graduate from boot camp. He had joined the navy. They also went to Disney World, where Meredith's sole desire was to get Mickey Mouse ears. Years later, she described it as the "highlight of my trip."

She and her father rode Space Mountain, the start of her love of roller coasters. Upside down, backward, over the top, any kind of roller coaster thrilled her. Her mother wouldn't get on any.

The next year, though, the Moons separated. Years of over-the-road truck driving had forged a permanent rift in their relationship. The breakup served as the start of a problem that followed Meredith into her teen years. She became insecure. She also began to have trouble trusting anyone.

After the divorce, Meredith lived for about a year in Norcross, Georgia, with her mother. But when her father moved to Rock Hill in 1992, Meredith wanted to go with him. She hadn't been particularly close to him until then, largely because he was absent so much of the time. Meredith was just starting high school. Douglas Moon continued to work for Ryder. Since he was traveling, Meredith stayed in a rented room with a woman who worked in the Ryder office. Then she moved in with another woman who rented rooms in her house, someone she had gotten to know through a civic program.

After Douglas Moon suffered a heart attack, he came off the road and rented a condominium at Brookside Manor in Rock Hill. Finally the two had a home of their own.

But Meredith was leading a double life. Her father thought her the dutiful daughter who came straight home from school and work. She was a member of the Northwestern High ROTC and was on a leadership track. She made good grades in honors classes.

Behind that veneer, she was actually a pot-smoking, hard-drinking girl. She had a pierced tongue, a ring in her left nipple and a tattoo of a peace sign on the outer side of her right ankle. Her left ear carried four earrings, her right five. She didn't run after boys, and boys certainly didn't run after her. She weighed almost three hundred pounds and was nearly six feet tall. She couldn't have cared less about boys, although she did have sex with a friend's brother during her high-school years. She gave him sex because she thought he would like her. Sex was not as interesting to her as getting high.

By tenth grade, she stopped caring about her weight because she had found marijuana. The first time she got high was not a result of peer pressure, but just the knowledge that other people were doing it. Because she smoked pot so much, people considered her a burnout. She didn't sell it, but other students came to her to find out where they could get it. That gave her a certain status in school, a status she enjoyed.

By her senior year, she was high every day. She never missed a day getting high. In fact, she'd smoke a joint or two at lunch.

"My eyes would be all red and people would say, 'Check out Meredith. She's high again.' I liked that," Moon said years later.

Chapter 10

Like most parents, Terry and Earl Robertson wanted only to raise their children to be upstanding citizens. And like many parents of their income and education level, they had the wherewithal to give them many things, to help them toward that goal.

Yet by 1994, Jimmy Robertson was out of control. He had a number of traffic violations, including speeding and shifting lanes improperly. In August of that year, Robertson was diagnosed as having bipolar disorder. His psychiatrist put him on Lithium therapy, which Robertson soon decided on his own was not effective. He quit taking the medication and his up-and-down mood swings and impulsive behavior resumed. He didn't sleep. He had ideas that he could accomplish anything and everything.

Chip Robertson, meanwhile, had graduated from Northwestern High and was headed to the University of Pennsylvania to study business. Earl and Terry could not have been prouder that one of their sons had been accepted to an Ivy League school, yet Chip had his own experiences with drugs and alcohol. Then he was diagnosed with attention deficit disorder (ADD), a condition characterized by an inability to pay attention. Children with the disorder often make careless mistakes and can't focus. They don't seem to listen and don't follow instructions well. They lose things, become restless and fidgety and often blurt out whatever comes to mind.

The doctor recommended the Robertsons put Chip on Ritalin, a stimulant that acts to normalize brain activity. He thought it would help him focus in his schoolwork. In patients with ADD, which amounts to about 5 percent of the population, it is generally believed that decreased activity in the brain causes inattention and an inability to focus. Ritalin was the wonder drug, the little pill that could tame a young boy and make a teacher's life more tolerable. Stimulants had been given to children with ADD since 1937.

When Chip Robertson started taking Ritalin, there was no talk of side effects or unintended behaviors or at least none that the Robertsons heard. They considered it a miraculous tool that would help their child realize his dreams, and theirs. There were no advocacy groups claiming that Ritalin and other psychotropic drugs caused children to behave violently. There were no school shootings in which the children doing the shooting were found to have been on Ritalin or Prozac or Luvox. There was no proposed legislation that would stop schools from requiring children with ADD to take their medication.

And there was no problem with young people who did not need the medication giving it or selling it to others to get high. It was not a drug that people abused.

The Robertsons felt that by putting their son on the medication, they were simply treating an illness. They followed their doctor's orders without fear or question. They wanted to do all they could to help their son succeed. They had no idea where it would lead.

After Jimmy Robertson flunked out of Georgia Tech, his father cut him off. He could live at home, but his health insurance, clothes and incidentals would have to come from his own earnings. Robertson enjoyed restaurants; in fact, he told a friend that "food service is my life." Still, he had trouble holding on to a job once he got it. He failed drug tests or had other problems on the job. His father did not approve of such blue-collar work, yet to the outside world Earl Robertson made it seem he was proud of both of his boys. He made sure his colleagues at Springs knew how bright the Robertson boys were.

In mid March 1995, Jimmy Robertson started therapy with Julius "Skip" Meyer, a psychologist in Rock Hill. During the hour-long first session, Robertson told him that he had an IQ of 140, that he never had much of a relationship with girls and that he had been sexually molested within the last year. He also said he was a chronic gambler.

Robertson continued therapy about every week for two months. In that time, Jimmy Robertson agreed to let his father handle his money. Their relationship seemed to improve, even to the point that Earl took his son with him to the storied Masters golf tournament in Augusta, Georgia.

By April, Meyer felt Robertson's relationship with his father had dramatically improved. In May, Robertson told the therapist he was thinking of going back to college. However, Meyer saw Robertson on an emergency basis a few days later and told him he needed to stay on Lithium.

Robertson saw Meyer only once in June but

returned for three visits in July. The up-and-down roller coaster that had become so much a part of Jimmy Robertson's life was noted and lamented by his mother and then shared with her friends. She loved to talk on the phone and regularly shared her concerns about her son with her friends. In July, she decided to start seeing Skip Meyer herself. She told her friends she was depressed and needed to talk to someone. She went twice a week initially and got to know the office manager there, Debbie Brisson, through her frequent visits. Sometimes Terry would fill in for her.

She told Meyer what her friends had told her: she was overprotective with her children and always felt it was her responsibility to keep the peace between Earl and the boys. She shared many of her concerns with her friends, but to her counselor, she was more open. Her friends had no idea that she was concerned that Earl had been unfaithful, that her mind raced and sometimes she thought of killing herself.

Terry Robertson had once been a slim blonde with a pleasing personality. She gained ten and then twenty, then more and more, until she was eighty pounds heavier than she had been just a short time before. A few years earlier, when a dashing Chip in his royal blue high-school graduation gown posed for pictures with his family, his mother sneaked behind him so she wouldn't look so heavy. Now she was even fatter.

Jimmy Robertson, who was twenty-one years of age, continued to see Meyer sporadically through the summer of 1995. In three visits in August, he told Meyer he was overwhelmed with life and depressed. On August 23, Robertson showed up at Meyer's office irate. He told the doctor he was "ready to have his mother arrested."

He was living at home with his parents, a college dropout with virtually no prospects, and was working unskilled jobs—jobs his father considered beneath his progeny. He had been arrested for driving under the influence (DUI) three times in six weeks.

Toward the end of August, Terry asked her son when he expected to make his rent payment. He railed at her to the point that she feared for her life. The usually docile Terry called the police. She told them her son abused alcohol and drugs and he had threatened her. But when police asked about filing charges, Terry decided against it. What would that help? she thought.

Instead, she sent the police to pick him up at work and take him to William S. Hall Psychiatric Institute in Columbia, a division of the state mental hospital. Robertson later told a doctor the police showed up at his workplace and said, "Come with us." It was an involuntary commitment based on Terry Robertson's belief that her son might harm her.

Ronald Prier, the associate director of adult inpatient therapy, treated him. He found Robertson was pleasant and cooperative but felt persecuted by his family, especially by his mother.

Robertson told the doctor he often went without sleep, sometimes getting only thirty minutes of sleep a night. He acted impulsively. His thoughts raced and he felt that he could be or do anything, things far beyond his actual capabilities.

He denied feeling homicidal or suicidal, the psychiatrist noted in his report.

"The psychological tests indicate a tremendous amount of aggression and acting out potential," William Rothstein, the chief of psychology service, wrote in his report. "He seems to have very poor emotional control."

Rothstein also found Robertson passive-aggressive, dependent and antisocial.

"Loss of anger control to the extent of harming others is a possibility," Rothstein wrote.

Prier gave Robertson a physical and found him in good shape except for a urinary tract infection. Robertson wouldn't let him examine his private parts. He also refused to attend any self-help groups until his parents came for family meeting night. Terry, Earl and Chip drove to Columbia for the family meeting. The doctor noted in his report that "a great deal of anger was expressed." Robertson's emotional turmoil had caused great stress not only for him but for the other three. His actions—bad checks, gambling, drugs—had caused financial problems for the family. They agreed, with the intercessions of the doctor, that Robertson needed to find someplace else to live.

During the week that Robertson was in the mental institution, he was housed in the Shearouse Pavilion and watched for signs of mania. None occurred. He also did not show any signs of feeling homicidal or suicidal, according to the doctor's report. The doctor noted that he repeatedly counseled Robertson about his dependence on alcohol.

Prier agreed with the earlier diagnosis that Robertson suffered from bipolar disorder and labeled his alcohol dependence severe. He also said his Axis IV diagnosis was mental illness with severe family strife. Prier changed his medication to Depakote. A condition such as bipolarity is stressful in itself, but the swirling emotions within the Robertson family made it especially troubling.

Later, Prier would say during testimony in Robertson's trial, "His family was understandably concerned about his potential to hurt somebody."

But that was information they did not share with their friends. No one had an inkling that doctors thought Robertson could be violent. And they most especially did not know he had actually shown violence toward his parents. The Robertsons lapsed into a state that other parents before them had been in with their children. They had a son they loved and he was troubled. They didn't know how to help him, though they had tried. They believed they were intelligent, competent people, yet this time they had no idea how to solve the problem. Doctors warned them, they didn't believe it could actually happen. This was Jimmy, who once was the adorable young boy whose smile radiated. And, anyway, what is a parent to do? Throw him out on the street? Some counselors advise parents to take action only when they have thought through everything that could possibly happen as a result. If they can live with the worst-case scenario, their action is warranted. Terry Robertson could not live with the worst that might happen to her son.

In December 1995, four months after Jimmy Robertson was admitted to the state mental hospital, Terry Robertson admitted herself. She had been expressing suicidal thoughts and had a counseling session with Skip Meyer on Thursday, November 30, and again on the following Monday and Tuesday. Meyer consulted with Dr. Hayne McMeekin, a psychiatrist who had been seeing Jimmy Robertson also, and Terry was told she'd be admitted involuntarily if she didn't go of her own free will.

She had been diagnosed as bipolar, the same illness

with which her son struggled. Her moods swung from high to low and she came to realize that some of her past behavior stemmed from the illness. When she stayed up all night working on PTA projects or bought items and never used them, it was classic mania, the high part of her emotions. When she felt like sleeping all day, she was on the low side of the cycle. Doctors also found her to be obsessive-compulsive. She believed that if she didn't do something a certain way, something bad would happen. She counted to fifty, over and over again.

Earl visited her in the hospital; the boys did not. She remained hospitalized for a little over two weeks. That left her barely four days to get ready for Christmas, a time she usually enjoyed. Through the years, she had collected any number of Christmas ornaments and decorations and she thrilled in the stringing of lights and hauling out the decorations, relishing the happy memories of favorite ornaments. In fact, Terry Robertson loved most holidays. She decorated for Easter and Thanksgiving. She bought cards for friends and family on Valentine's Day and the Fourth of July, but this year she couldn't recapture the Christmas spirit. That added to her already overpowering guilt for all the problems of her family.

In February, Earl and Terry were still fighting over whether they should force their son to move out. They had all agreed back in August, when Jimmy Robertson was hospitalized, that he should find his own place to live. Seven months later, the argument continued. Earl was prepared to make the break. Terry's friends encouraged her that it was the best thing for all concerned.

Chapter 11

Not long before he was involuntarily admitted to the mental hospital, Jimmy Robertson met Meredith Moon, who was a friend of Erin Savage's, the girl he had been dating for about a month.

Robertson met them at Sagebrush Steakhouse in Rock Hill. He seemed hyper, nervous. At one point, Savage left the table to go to the bathroom. Robertson told Moon he had bought tickets to see the rock group REM for Savage's birthday. He made her promise not to tell Savage, but in the way of teenage girls, she could hardly wait to do so. Robertson was furious and continued to berate her about it for years.

Moon saw that smoldering anger again when Savage told him a guy at work had been harassing her. Robertson, Moon and Savage went to a Waffle House that a friend worked at. Robertson had his friend empty the grease trap into a plastic bag. He drove over to Paces River, an apartment complex, and found the car of the man Savage said had been harassing her. He poured the grease over the car and slashed the tires, Moon said.

Robertson continued working blue-collar jobs, just as he continued smoking pot and abusing alcohol. His bad driving record grew longer: running red lights, failure to pay tickets. In February 1996, he was cited for operating an unsafe vehicle and failing to pay a ticket. He told Meyer how his father called him "stupid" and chided him for making bad decisions. Robertson got four more tickets in March, including a charge of driving with a suspended license.

Terry's friends knew she was having trouble with depression, but they figured who wouldn't with sons as messed up as Jimmy and Chip. She did not tell her friends, but life with Earl had become unbearable. They barely spoke. She wasn't interested in his golf or work. She certainly didn't want sex. And she didn't trust him. She thought he was too tough on the boys and she wondered if he had had affairs with other women. He flirted with other women, she thought. About the only area she felt confident in his abilities was that of provider. He made a good living and she never had to think about working. Sometimes she wondered if they should just end their marriage.

Responding to a suggestion from her counselor, whom she was still seeing a couple times a week, Terry started doing more with her friends. One night they enjoyed live music at the Hereford Barn Steakhouse in Charlotte. They went shopping. She cooked dinner once or twice a week.

Also at Meyer's suggestion she read *Motherless Daughters,* a book published two years before that detailed women's reactions and grief over losing their mothers. After six years, she still couldn't shake the loss of her mother. The book helped her understand her feelings.

But her worries about her eldest son compounded in May when she discovered he had stolen some of her checks. He cashed one for $200. She worried about what he was using the money for—she guessed alcohol—and she worried about what Earl was going to do if he found out.

Earl and Terry thought they had convinced Chip to stay away from Jimmy, that Jimmy would only get his brother in trouble. They found out midsummer that Chip had not. Earl Robertson, the strong provider, decided he needed counseling. He started to see Skip Meyer in June 1996. He went at his wife's request, he told the counselor.

He had multiple sources of frustration. He worked hard—had worked all his life, for that matter—and saved money. Still, he had a poor relationship with his wife, who didn't keep house or cook, and his two sons, who didn't respect him. What he really wanted to do was play golf. At times, he felt like he wanted to go to sleep and not wake up.

In July, Jimmy Robertson broke into the next-door neighbor's house. When police arrested him, he signed a confession saying he broke into the house early on a Saturday morning, July 20, 1996. He said he gained entry by breaking the latch on a living-room window and put socks over his hands so he did not leave fingerprints. He systematically moved through the house, back to front, gathering goods he knew he could sell. He returned the next day for more.

The Robertsons discovered that Jimmy was using crack. They also learned that Chip was using drugs as well.

Robertson was sentenced in a courtroom at the Moss Justice Center.

His parents were mortified. How could they face their friends, much less the next-door neighbor? They began to withdraw from activities. Earl's coworkers thought he tended to stay in his office more, wasn't quite as chatty or outgoing. They quit going to Sunday school and church. Even though Terry continued to talk with her friends on the phone every day, she held back in telling them everything she was feeling and everything that was happening. As time passed, she didn't talk about the family at all. She stayed home more and more and sometimes wouldn't get out of bed. Her main source of comfort was the oldies radio station from Charlotte, which played the songs of her college years, a time when life was so much easier.

When Linda Weaver would call and insist on getting her out of the house for lunch, Terry would reluctantly go, but there were certain restaurants she wouldn't frequent because she was afraid she'd run into someone. Sometimes she wouldn't go to the grocery store, and when she did, she would peek down the aisles to see if anyone she knew was there. She did not want to face people she knew. Embarrassment ruled her life. The idea that her firstborn was in prison was more than she could bear. She was humiliated by his behavior and its reflection on her as a parent, but she also worried about his safety. She knew about the degradation that went on in prison. She had seen enough television shows to know prison was not a safe place for a slightly built, blond and blue-eyed young man.

But on some level, parents of an alcoholic and drug-abusing child have some comfort in the child being imprisoned. They know where their child is, and they hope it will be the bottom everyone's been telling them the child has to hit before a life changes. It is also a relief that the child—and his problems— no longer slaps the parent in the face at every turn. And that, too, brings guilt.

Guilt is the active emotion for parents of troubled

children. Terry and Earl Robertson were no different from any other parent who suffered with a child in trouble. They worried about what they did to cause their child to act in such a way. Terry Robertson especially felt she had messed up her children. She believed she had been a bad mother and a bad wife.

And as her depression grew, life itself grew more and more difficult. Her house was a mess. Her body was fat. She bought items at the store, brought them home and never took them out of the bag. Books, left unread, piled up on her nightstand. Her medicine cabinet overflowed with prescription drugs. Sometimes she took her medication for bipolar disorder and sometimes she didn't.

Jimmy Robertson was sent to Lee Correctional Institution in Bishopville, South Carolina, a town on the opposite side of the state from Rock Hill. It was the only state prison with an extensive inpatient drug rehabilitation program. He had a month of counseling in prison in October.

His parents spent a despondent Christmas with him in prison, while Chip was drinking too much and smoking pot. They worried he was headed straight down the same road as his older brother. Terry believed Chip had a distinct drinking problem. Jimmy, meanwhile, attended Narcotics Anonymous, prison records show. His parents visited him about once a month to once every two months. It was not a pleasant ride for the parents. Earl resented going. He resented having to explain to people that he had a son in jail. None of his relationships were working out. Even his relationship with his mother was strained. To him, she seemed overly critical and that was something he certainly did not need.

Earl felt overwhelmed by the circumstances of his life and hopeless that it would ever be better. His life was nothing like he had dreamed, nothing like he had planned, but he felt he had done what he was supposed to do. He also believed no one cared what he thought or felt. He had failed.

Jimmy Robertson took a stress and anger management class in June 1997 at Lee. In a self-analysis questionnaire he completed as part of the class, he said he felt anxious waiting for elevators, sometimes felt grouchy or irritable and became irritated by teenagers who blared loud music and wore odd clothes and hairstyles. He acknowledged he counted how many items people in front of him in the express checkout line were buying and that he raised his voice in an argument.

He also wondered why obese people couldn't control their food intake or exercise more. It was not lost on him that his mother, who once was a slim, attractive young girl, had put on quite a bit of weight—eighty pounds, maybe more.

He also said in the questionnaire that he felt using profanity with relatives helped express his feelings better. He scored in the high range for distrust and forcefulness and very high for aggravation. In his notes, he wrote his number one action to curb his anger was to look for win/win situations. The second: respect needs of others.

The very stress management booklet on which he listed his own feelings was used again some months later. The night he killed his parents, someone wrote on the back of the booklet: "Alarm clock, wipe downstairs doorknob, dispose of yard rake."

Chapter 12

Chip Robertson came home for the summer of 1997, a development his parents met with anxiety. Even though life was not perfect with just the two of them in the house, it was so much easier than dealing with the problems of a young adult. Chip would turn twenty-one in September, the age of majority. He had been drinking alcohol for some time; now he would be legal.

A few weeks before Jimmy Robertson was released from prison, his father found out he might be promoted and transferred to Mexico City. In many ways, the idea was irresistible. A new start in an exotic locale. To Terry, it was all too reminiscent of moving to France when she was a child. She also worried about how her son was going to fare in the outside world. She believed he was incapable of coping with society's expectations.

Robertson was released from prison the last day of July 1997. He had been imprisoned almost a year. His record inside was not spotless. He had been involved in a fight, although the prison record is not clear whether he was fighting or being beaten up.

His path crossed Meredith's once again after he was released. Erin Savage was out of the picture. Her parents emphatically told her to stay away from him. Before he went to prison, he had called her repeatedly, to the point of obsession. Savage's father confronted Robertson and told him to leave his daughter alone.

Moon had no such intercessor. Her father did not even know she was spending any time with Jimmy Robertson other than at work. They were both working in the food court at Winthrop University. Sometimes Robertson worked for days on end, twelve hours a day. Once he worked twenty-seven days straight.

His parents were adamant that he find his own place to live. He located a place through an advertisement in the newspaper. He moved into a room in the Rock Hill apartment of Darren Keller. Earl Robertson gave Keller the first month's rent and a security deposit. It was a relief for the Robertsons that their son was not coming home. They were anxious about his release. Their lives had taken on a more normal hue in the months Jimmy was in prison and Chip was in college at the University of Pennsylvania.

Earl Robertson was particularly embarrassed by his son's prison term and did not talk or joke around as much with coworkers. Earl Robertson, the Eagle Scout, still could not fathom that his son would steal from the next-door neighbor.

Besides the guilt Terry felt over her son's mental illness, she also struggled with the same feelings as many middle-aged women. She was months away from fifty with no job and two grown sons who were having a tough time making it in the world, yet she couldn't help them. She needed to be needed. No one needed her anymore.

Moon practically moved into Keller's apartment

with Robertson. She wasn't sure what Robertson wanted from her or what the future would hold. She couldn't even describe their relationship adequately to her friends. It was more than causal. More than sex. More than drugs. They were together all the time, though they never actually went on dates. It was Moon's first serious relationship. She was eighteen; he was almost twenty-four. The age difference meant nothing to her. It meant nothing to Robertson, either. For most of his life, Robertson had felt he had more in common with people five years or so younger than himself.

Sometimes Moon would daydream that she and Robertson would marry one day. He was handsome and smart and fun. He loved drugs and alcohol, just as she did.

It did not cross Moon's mind that he had no serious job or an education that would help him qualify for one. All she knew was they were having fun. There were plenty of drugs, and he was old enough to buy liquor. Robertson saw himself as good-time Jimmy, the perennial host whose responsibility was to make sure everyone had a great time.

Keller's apartment soon turned into playland against his wishes. People came in and out at all hours. Robertson and his friends were drinking and drugging. One night, Moon drank most of a bottle of Jägermeister. She passed out on the bathroom floor. Panicked, Robertson called Erin Savage to help her.

Terry Robertson knew how much her sons were drinking and desperately tried to get them to Alcoholics Anonymous. They refused. What she didn't know was that they had started abusing Ritalin, which they got from Chip's prescription. They would crush it up and snort it like cocaine.

In August, Terry Robertson seemed to come out of her depression. She had been seeing a psychiatrist and counselor for more than a year. Her friends saw her more often and she reported to them she had taken a stand with her sons. No more intercessor. She was trying to mend her broken relationship with her husband, but Earl still felt unappreciated and misunderstood. His wife's mood swings unsettled him. He wanted continuity and stability. Sleep became his escape.

The next month, Earl and Terry Robertson took a trip to New England. Few things in life can provide a sense that God is in control than a New England fall. The reds of the sugar maples and the yellows of the birches create a glow unmatched in nature except by the setting sun itself. Terry was feeling so vibrant, she even let Earl take her picture at the top of Mount Washington in the White Mountains of New Hampshire.

In October, Earl went to Philadelphia to see Chip. He learned Chip hadn't been to class for two weeks. Drinking ruled his life and he was about to be kicked out of school. Earl became angry.

Then the next month, Keller asked Jimmy Robertson to leave his apartment. Keller was particularly concerned about the drug use taking place there. He worried he might lose the apartment and possibly even be arrested. He had wanted to ask Robertson to leave for weeks, but he had been putting it off. Finally he did it and Robertson made plans to return home with his parents.

Earl was angry and resented the fact that his twenty-four-year-old son could not hold it together enough to live independently. He felt he was always the fall guy, that his wife in particular made him out to be the bad guy. Meanwhile, all he felt he was doing was disciplining the boys. His sons ruined his life, causing him to feel hopeless. Nothing would ever be better.

Part 3
The Trial

Chapter 13

Courtrooms and theaters have much in common. Actors work for favor from an audience, lawyers a jury. The opponents—the prosecution and the defense—advance their cases precisely, delicately, to engage the twelve jurors, to get them to believe only them. The state versus James D. Robertson would match Sixteenth Circuit solicitor Thomas Pope, known universally as Tommy, and an assistant solicitor, Kevin Brackett, with local criminal defense attorneys William Hancock and James Boyd.

Pope was already well known far beyond York County, South Carolina. He was the prosecutor who sent Susan Smith to prison for killing her sons, Michael, three, and Alex, eighteen months. On a dark October night, Smith released the hand brake of her blue Honda Accord and let the car roll into the cold water of John D. Long Lake in Union, South Carolina, with her sons strapped in car seats inside. Smith then ran to a nearby house and said a black man had jumped into her car at a red light, shoved her out and driven off with her sons.

Her lie resounded across America as people became riveted to the story of the young mother grieving for her lost boys and pleading on national television for their safe return. Nine days later, Smith's story unraveled and she directed Sheriff Howard Wells of Union County to her children's bodies at the bottom of the murky lake.

Pope sought the death penalty for Smith, but the jury could not find its way to sentence the troubled young woman to death. It was Pope's second death penalty case, his first loss.

Pope was a local boy. He grew up on a farm southeast of Rock Hill, much like the one he owned as a husband and father. His father was a deputy sheriff who was elected sheriff the year the son graduated from high school. His grandfather was a doctor on the Catawba Indian Reservation.

Sheriff Pope gave his son a bit of advice: don't go into law enforcement. Tommy Pope headed to the University of South Carolina in Columbia, seventy miles south of Rock Hill. But once in the dorm, he realized he needed something to occupy his hours outside of class.

"I didn't have a lot of self-restraint," he said, remembering freedom's enticements. He took a job as the phone boy at the State Law Enforcement Division and virtually lived at the agency's headquarters, dispatching bloodhounds and homicide detectives. Sometimes he'd tag along with the narcotics agents. He looked at the agents as if they were superheroes, doling out truth, justice and the American way. He calls it "getting blue lights in your veins."

When he graduated from Carolina, he went to work full-time for SLED as an agent. Legendary chief of the State Law Enforcement Division J. P. Strom gave him his first badge and became his mentor. Strom encouraged him to go to law school.

"He saw something in me that I didn't see myself," Pope said.

Pope graduated from University of South Carolina School of Law in December 1987, a semester earlier than his peers. He just wanted out of school. Terminally ill with cancer, his mother died the next month. He believes she "stretched it out" to see him graduate. She was always the parent who encouraged his studies. She was a college graduate in a time when few women even graduated high school. At forty, his mother went to college and earned a master's degree and worked as a teacher. Pope's father did not graduate from high school.

Pope landed a job as an assistant prosecutor in Lexington County, South Carolina, the adjacent county to the west of Columbia's Richland County. He worked for Donnie Myers, who was known in South Carolina as the king of the death penalty. "Dr. Death," folks called him. He had sent more men to death row than any other prosecutor in the state. He rarely lost.

Pope prosecuted drug cases for three years there; then York County solicitor Larry Grant called and asked if he'd be interested in working for him. Pope wasn't, but the solicitation started him thinking about living in Rock Hill again. In 1991, Pope went to work for the York County Sheriff's Office as an undercover narcotics detective.

Two months later, his wife left him and took his son back to Columbia.

Pope was twenty-nine.

He decided to run for solicitor against Grant. "I figured I couldn't do any worse. The backlog was the worst in the state," Pope said. He won the election of 1992 with 55 percent of the vote.

Pope viewed his work as a calling. When he frequently said his role was to see justice done, he stated it with such unabashed sincerity that it didn't sound hokey or pumped up. "We're dealing with people's lives and it's not a numbers game," he has said.

His first death penalty case was in 1993, which he won.

The next year, Susan Smith murdered her sons. Pope had just remarried in July, and his son was four, a year older than Michael Smith. His son said to him one day, "Daddy, a bad thing has happened. That woman killed her children."

The Smith case, though, became more than a woman killing her children.

"Nothing can prepare you for that," Pope said of the media circus that ensued during the June 1995 trial. Now, he also realizes he was naive in not understanding the power of the anti-death-penalty factions even in a state like South Carolina, where the death penalty is overwhelmingly accepted as proper punishment for all manner of murders.

By the time the trial was over, it was widely accepted that Susan Smith wasn't merely a cold, calculating child killer, but a victim herself. She had been used or abused by almost every man in her life, most especially by her stepfather, with whom she had had oral sex as a teenager and with whom she had continued a relationship after she was a married woman and mother.

Pope was criticized for seeking death for Smith. Eight years later, when interviewed for the book, he still bristled at the subject. He believes if a black man in a toboggan or David Smith, the children's father, had been on trial and he had not sought the ultimate penalty, he'd have been criticized even more harshly. He also believes they'd have been sent to death row.

Pope keeps a framed picture of Michael and Alex Smith on a bookcase in his office at the Moss Justice Center, as well as a picture of him with David Smith. He has a corner office on the second floor decorated with an imposing modular desk cabinet unit and simple straight-back chairs. He keeps mementos of other trials around also, including a white hat, which a victim gave him, and his father's badge. A large drawing of an elephant takes up one wall. He registered as a Republican when he ran for office, even though he considers law enforcement his party. He figured if he's ever voted out of office by a Democrat, the picture will end up in the trash and he can take it home with him.

Kevin Brackett served as second chair in the Robertson case. Brackett's background could not be more different from Pope's. Where Pope had the gregariousness of a country lawyer, Brackett was serious and demure.

Brackett was born in Japan and lived all over the world: the Philippines, Thailand, England, Spain, Colorado, Texas, Maryland, Florida and South Carolina. His father, originally from Rock Hill, was an officer in the air force. The longest the family stayed in one place was three years. He remembers it as a difficult time. He was the youngest of three children and he felt no sense of roots, no continuity to his life. When it came time for college, he chose the University of South Carolina because it would be free. His father's great uncle had established a trust fund for all descendants to attend any South Carolina college they desired. It paid for law school, too. He worked as a bartender and clerked for a public defender for spending money during law school.

He had dreamed of being a doctor, but the harder high-school math and science classes convinced him his future career was something else. Clerking for the public defender showed him the intrigue and challenges of trial work. He knew that was where he wanted to work. His was hired as an assistant solicitor in York County the year before Pope was elected. Trial work appealed to him especially because it almost always ended with a resolution. Life is not so clear-cut. In a trial, the prosecution presents its case, the defense its case and the jury decides who's right. It's tidy.

Chapter 14

Meredith Moon had agreed to be sent back to South Carolina in January 1998. To her, there was never a choice to make. She told herself she had two options: the easy way or the hard way. She also desperately wanted to see her family. She had spent Thanksgiving and Christmas alone in a jail cell in Philadelphia. She wanted to go home. She chose the easy way, which to her meant helping the authorities.

Ralph Misle, the York County Sheriff's Office homicide detective, drove with a female SLED agent to Philadelphia to bring her back. He was surprised to see Moon had slimmed down, probably lost fifteen pounds in the few months since he had seen her last. She was wearing the same clothes she had on when she was arrested, except the sweater. The brown corduroy pants were too big and she had no belt. She also had on a white T-shirt with a blue T-shirt on top.

Not long after they left the jail, Misle stopped and bought her a pack of Marlboro Menthol Lights, some chips and a diet Coke. Her hands were handcuffed in front of her, making smoking difficult, but she managed to burn through the whole pack.

He asked her about her involvement. What was she doing when Robertson was doing this or that?

He asked her about putting socks on her hands. Moon said she didn't want to answer any more questions without an attorney present. He said OK and stopped the questioning.

When they stopped to eat at Wendy's, Misle slipped the handcuffs off.

"If you run, I'll have to shoot you," he said.

A week after her return to South Carolina and her incarceration at the York County Detention Center, Moon's parents visited. As soon as the jailer opened the door for her to go into the inmate side of the visiting room, she began to cry. Through a Plexiglas window via telephone, Moon made small talk. She didn't want to have a serious conversation with them. She was glad to see them but also could see disappointment etched on their faces.

Robertson sat through Christmas, New Year's Day and on into February in Philadelphia, fighting attempts to send him back to South Carolina. He wrote letters to his brother, pleading with him to hire a lawyer for him.

"This is a terrible tragedy, but what's done is done," Robertson wrote to Chip. "And maybe one day we will all know the real truth—not just what the media or DA's office thinks is the truth."

He wanted a "top-notch" attorney, and told Chip he had interviewed some from jail. One would cost about $175,000. A later letter informed Chip another lawyer could be secured for much less, $75,000. But Chip did not answer. Robertson wrote to Eugene "Gene" Sullivan, a financial adviser who was handling the estate. He wanted to know why Chip wasn't writing. He last talked to him just before Christmas.

Robertson also wrote to his former neighbor Beth Langley. He told her he missed his mom and dad and said they all had just started getting along when they died. He was considering taking his own life, he said. Then he asked her about the new Pearl Jam album and wondered how Skip Meyer and Hayne McMeekin, the family's psychologist and psychiatrist, respectively, were taking the news of his parents' deaths. He asked her to send him copies of articles written about the case.

In mid January, Robertson wrote to Chip: "Regardless of your decision or what side you choose to stand on, we will still be brothers and I will always love you."

Chip Robertson did not go back to college. He spent Thanksgiving with his parents' friends, and after the funerals, he spent a few days with his grandmother in Georgia. Then he moved back into the house on Westminster. He regularly entertained. On New Year's Eve, his friends told police he had a party that grew louder and louder as the evening progressed and morning came. Some of the guests went upstairs to see the blood spatters still on the wall. It was not until February that the upstairs was cleaned up by a forensic cleaning company at a cost of about $9,500.

His parents' wills were filed in York County Probate Court in mid December. The estate was being held in abeyance until it became clear Chip Robertson would not be implicated. He was given a modest allowance and his regular monthly bills—the mortgage on the Rock Hill house and the house his parents owned in Michigan, cable television and lawn care service—were paid. Terry and Earl Robertson had identical

wills, which named the other as executor and benefi-
ciary and their children as beneficiaries should the
parents die at the same time. The wills had been written in 1983, not long after they returned to Rock Hill
and bought their home on Westminster. They named
Terry's parents executors and guardians of the children. Since they had both died, the executor became
NationsBank.

In one of those bizarre life coincidences, the work
for the bank fell in part to Sally Skardon, Terry
Robertson's college friend and, in 1997, a trust officer for NationsBank. She and another trust officer
arrived at the house shortly after the murders, getting necessary papers and securing the valuables.
Gene Sullivan and Chip Robertson met them there.
As Skardon went through the house, she imagined
how grim life had become for her once-vibrant
friend. The house was a mess and prescription drugs
filled the cabinet. Retrieved for safekeeping were
some 82 pieces of Terry Robertson's jewelry, Earl
Robertson's 754 baseball cards and some silver
Christmas ornaments. The items were stored in the
NationsBank vault.

At the end of February, Robertson lost his fight
against extradition, and SLED agents drove him back
to York County. When he arrived at the Moss Justice
Center, which houses the county jail and courtrooms
as well as the solicitor's office, he appeared weary and
withdrawn. He wore a T-shirt and pants as he shuffled
into the detention center shackled at wrist and ankle.

At his bond hearing ten days later, Robertson
stood before circuit court judge John C. Hayes III in
jail orange. He glared at Pope and did not take his
eyes from him except to address the judge.

Hayes had been a circuit court judge in York County for seven years. Like most judges in South Carolina, who are appointed by the general assembly, he was a legislator at the time of his appointment. He served in the South Carolina House of Representatives from 1981 to 1984 and had served in the state senate since 1985. Hayes also served as chairman of the South Carolina Coastal Council, which set state policy on matters involving the booming South Carolina coast, and served as chairman of the York County Delegation for the seven years before he became a judge.

He enjoyed his work as a judge and had the idea that one day he'd write about his experiences.

Pope told the judge he "most likely" intended to seek the death penalty against Robertson. Hayes, as expected, denied bail. Robertson would be represented by court-appointed lawyers William "Bill" Hancock and James Boyd, two longtime criminal defense attorneys. His parents' estate was not available to him.

Like Pope, Boyd was a Rock Hill native. He grew up in the Mount Holly community an only child, raised by his mother and grandfather. James Boyd's father died when Boyd was eight and his grandmother when he was ten. Like Pope and Brackett, he was a graduate of the University of South Carolina, both the undergraduate school and the law school. He thought for a time he might go into some sort of government work, social services or the state department. He majored in government, but in his senior year he chose the law.

After graduating from law school in 1977, Boyd worked for about three years in a general law firm in

Rock Hill. He handled criminal and civil cases as well as real estate matters. In 1981, he became York County's first public defender, a job he held for about six years until he opened a private practice.

In the courtroom, he had the same folksy manner as Pope, with a slow Southern pattern to his speech. But he didn't have the showmanship of Pope, who was about ten years younger. Boyd had been practicing law for two decades when he was appointed to the Robertson case. He joined Hancock on the case after public defender Harry Dest opted out because he had already agreed to represent Moon. It was Boyd's sixth death penalty case. He had saved the lives of all but the first one, Sylvester Adams, who had kidnapped and strangled a teenage neighbor. When Adams insisted on testifying, he made bizarre, nonsensical comments from the witness stand. The last death penalty case Boyd worked was against Pope.

Death penalty cases never got easier. Everyone was different. Plus, the responsibility of defending someone's life—in effect holding their life in his hands—remained forever awesome.

In the Robertson case, he knew the odds of a not guilty verdict were slim. The evidence was overwhelming. He described it as a slam dunk case for the prosecution, but he felt some measure of confidence in getting him a life sentence because juries tended to hesitate before giving death sentences in cases involving family members. He intended to bring witnesses who would say Terry and Earl Robertson would not have wanted their son to be executed.

Hancock and Boyd knew the odds were long. Robertson seemed to have planned the murders and to cover it up afterward, not the signs of a mentally ill person. It would be difficult to explain how a son could do something that gruesome to his parents.

Robertson was sent for safekeeping to Lee Correctional, where he had served his burglary sentence. But in November, his attorneys petitioned the court for him to be brought back to York County. The distance of 240 miles, round-trip, proved a hardship, they argued. Hayes agreed.

They had won another victory from the judge the month before when Hayes ruled they could have copies of the counseling records of Terry and Earl Robertson. Friends of the family knew Terry had been seeing Skip Meyer, a Rock Hill therapist. Few knew Earl had seen him as well. Meyer, who earned his doctorate from the University of Florida, fought releasing the records, saying he feared it would set a precedent and would cause patients to worry that they could not speak freely.

But Hancock argued the information in the records would give Robertson's attorneys information they needed if they were to launch an insanity defense.

"I don't believe we can show the court any better cause than a man fighting for his life," Hancock told Hayes.

The news story about the judge granting access to the records caught some friends of the family off guard, but they had no idea what the defense attorneys were about to learn—and tell the world—about the Robertson family.

Chapter 15

Robertson was a model prisoner in the months he waited to stand trial. Initially the trial was scheduled to begin February 1, 1999, more than a year after Earl and Terry Robertson were murdered. But in January, defense attorneys wanted to run DNA tests on blood samples in evidence, delaying the trial six weeks. The next month, Hayes ordered Robertson to submit to psychiatric testing for the state.

In the year he was jailed, Robertson had regular visits from friends, a cousin, a church member and Sullivan, the family's financial counselor. He wrote memo after memo to Ralph Misle, who had been promoted to jail director. The memos were written in the vein of a corporate executive asking for help from a colleague. Robertson asked for books by John Grisham, Scott Turow and Jonathan Kellerman. He wrote to the prison director about visitation: "My family is limited due to the deaths of my parents," his correspondence began.

Another correspondence he sent was to Moon. "Go fuck yourself," it read. That was all Moon needed to decide she would help the prosecutor fully. She would do anything to help herself but also to see Robertson get what he deserved. It was an emotional and psychological turning point for Moon, who felt at one point so tied to Robertson she would do anything for him or anything he said.

She was also beginning to understand her role in the deaths of his parents. The law in South Carolina says that "the hand of one is the hand of all." No matter she did not grasp a hammer, swing a bat or wield a knife, she was an accomplice. Charged with two counts of murder and facing the death penalty, just as Robertson was, she felt remorse. She was haunted by the fact she did not help the Robertsons. It took her a year to realize her culpability and that Robertson, this man whom she had thought for a time she would marry, was only out for himself.

Pope framed his case on the belief that Robertson was a greedy, spoiled son, unwilling to wait for his share of a $2 million inheritance. Earl and Terry Robertson's wills had been submitted to probate court and in the June 1998 inventory of Earl's net worth, it showed Earl's estate to be valued at $1.5 million, nearly half of which were life insurance policies that Jimmy and Chip Robertson would, under normal circumstances, have benefited from. Terry's estate was valued at $641,000. The inventories listed as beneficiary: to be determined.

The house was valued at nearly $200,000. An entry of $4,959.21 was itemized as "Springs Industries final paycheck." Earl Robertson was also given a $10,000 bonus and had three IRAs totaling nearly $40,000. Their savings accounts amounted to about $5,000 and stocks had a value of about $250,000. Terry's jewelry was valued at about $16,000 and her 1989 Cadillac $650. Her life insurance was worth $150,000.

However it was itemized, it was a lot of money to a twenty-four-year-old who truly had no real concept of money.

Three hundred York County residents were called to the Moss Justice Center for jury duty during the week of James D. Robertson's long-awaited trial. The court asked 160 of them to come on the first day, March 15, 1999. The courtroom was full of spectators, mainly with people who did not know the Robertsons. The Weavers and, along with other longtime friends, the Turners had asked for special consideration to be treated as family so they could sit in the courtroom for the entire trial. They were on the witness list, to be called during the penalty phase if Robertson was convicted. Ordinarily, witnesses cannot hear other testimony and Hayes was not of the mind to grant the friends family status.

A film crew from Court TV was in the courtroom, videotaping the proceedings for airing at a later date. Oddly, subscribers to local cable television would not be able to see the Court TV coverage, since that was not a channel the local company subscribed to. Local television and print reporters watched attentively as Robertson strode into the courtroom. Carrying papers in his left hand, he wore gray slacks, a blue oxford cloth shirt, striped tie and a navy blue blazer. His hair was neatly combed. He looked every bit the Georgia Tech collegian he once was.

The first day took twelve hours and eleven of the forty people needed for the jury pool were accepted. Jurors were asked whether they knew of the case or any of the people expected to testify. They also were asked whether they could sentence someone to die. On the first day, two said they could not

give the death penalty for any reason and two said
they could vote for death but could not sign the
death warrant. All four were excused.

"I've never had to face decisions like this before,"
one woman told a local newspaper.

After a break, Robertson, Pope and Brackett had
returned to the courtroom. Boyd and Hancock were
not there yet and Judge Hayes was clearly ready to
resume.

"I can question the witness," Robertson said,
standing.

Observers thought it seemed he was enjoying the
show, the attention. It was as if he did not actually
grasp his part in the drama.

At the end of the third day, six men, six women,
and two alternates were chosen to decide whether
Robertson murdered his parents, and if he did
whether he deserved to die.

Hayes had denied a defense motion to seat a jury
from outside of York County because of pretrial pub-
licity. He wrote by hand specific instructions for the
jury, which was to be sequestered. Members were to
report to the jury room at 9:30 on Thursday morning. They could not bring radios, CDs, televisions,
cell phones, beepers, weapons, illegal drugs, alcoholic beverages, computer games of violence or
reading material on trials, murder, capital punishment or religion. They could bring a computer to be
used without an Internet connection in the common
rooms.

Chapter 16

Before testimony began in the Robertson case on Thursday morning, the prosecution had business. Meredith Moon was allowed to plead guilty to reduced charges in return for her testimony against Robertson. She had been charged with two counts of murder, as Robertson was, and could have faced the death penalty as well. South Carolina has only sent one woman in modern history to death row. Years after the state fashioned a death row at Women's Correctional Institution in Columbia, her sentence was overturned.

The arrest warrant accused Moon of murdering Terry Robertson. But that Thursday morning, Deputy Solicitor Brackett told Hayes that Moon had been asked to the Robertson home by James Robertson. He told her when she arrived he was going to kill his parents and then the two of them would go to Philadelphia. She heard the murder, but she did not take part.

"Is that account accurate?" Hayes asked Moon.

"Yes, sir," said Moon, wearing a blue dress and yellow sweater. Jail had served as her diet plan. In the fifteen months since her arrest, she had lost more than one hundred pounds. She was proud of the way she looked. In the months since the murders, Moon had done a lot of thinking, a lot of soul searching. She heard Terry Robertson's screams over and over. She was consumed with guilt that she did not run for help when she learned what Robertson intended to do. She could not explain her actions. She had no answer when her parents or the prosecutors or anybody asked why she did not flee. She was smoking a cigarette outside. She had a car, and yet she stayed, paralyzed. Fear? Love? What kept her there?

With her parents standing behind her, Moon pleaded guilty to two counts of accessory after the fact of murder. Then she pleaded guilty to armed robbery, and as she did, she started to cry.

She said later, "I knew I was guilty of the accessory, so I did not have any trouble paying my dues in that respect, but it was hard for me to plead guilty to armed robbery. It was either take that or take that with murder and a trial. There was no choice for me there."

She faced twenty to sixty years in prison, but sentencing was delayed until after Robertson's trial was over.

After Moon's plea, Robertson came into the courtroom. He wore a blue blazer, khaki pants, a white shirt and a green striped tie. As was his custom, after he sat down in the mauve upholstered chair at the defense table, he turned to look at the audience. He had a slight grin on his face as if he were a celebrity looking at adoring fans.

Pope began with a seven-minute opening statement.

"Ladies and gentlemen, you've already been through a difficult process and I'll be honest with you, it's just beginning. I'll apologize in advance for the case you're about to see, but the state does intend to bear its burden and the state does intend to bring the evidence forward to you," he said, his voice moderated and conversational, his words measured and precise.

He reminded jurors that they were, as the judge had already told them, in the guilt phase of the trial and that punishment was not anything they should be concerned with.

"So, now the issue you have before you is can the state prove beyond a reasonable doubt that this defendant," he said, looking at jurors but pointing behind him toward Robertson, seated beside his attorneys, "murdered both his parents. That he took a credit card from his father's wallet and other items of personal property, went and used that credit card in part to facilitate his escape and in part of facilitating his alibi because what you will discover from the evidence presented is that early on that Tuesday, right before Thanksgiving, Tuesday the twenty-fifth, Terry Dejarnette Robertson, who had a number of close friends, was supposed to be certain places at certain times."

He told jurors they would hear testimony from the friends Terry was supposed to meet, that they missed her, and from coworkers who would tell about Earl not showing up for work.

"This is really the problem with Jim's plan, because the plan was to make it look like a burglary that takes both the parents' lives: Jim, Meredith Moon, the other brother, Chip, come back from school and find somebody broke in and killed Mom and Dad. What they didn't count on was Terry and Earl having so many close friends."

Two hours after the crime, the friends are calling each other, worried.

The testimony will trace his route, Pope said, from the house to the Peach Stand to Ladysmith, Virginia, to Philadelphia, Pennsylvania, where they're arrested. In Maryland, they put an odd assortment of items in a Dumpster: a bat, a hammer, a knife, checks, bloody clothes and socks worn over the hands to prevent fingerprints.

"The truth be known, if Meredith Moon had not told the police in Philadelphia that evidence may never have been recovered," he said.

He told the jury they would have all the evidence they needed to convict.

Robertson's attorney Bill Hancock began his opening statement by telling jurors, "I remind you that what I say is not evidence. As we course through this trial, the way it takes place is the solicitor presents his witnesses and is allowed to cross-examine and to test the credibility of those witnesses. The judge has told you he is the sole authority of the law. You are to take the law as he explains it to you."

He explained the jurors' role as finders of fact and reiterated the state's responsibility for proving guilt beyond a reasonable doubt. He explained the defense's reasons for objecting to testimony as stemming from a desire that the rules be followed, not as a way to hide evidence.

"Don't hold any of those objections against Jimmy Robertson sitting here," Hancock said, motioning toward Robertson as he walked over and stood directly in front of the defendant. Robertson looked on, expressionless.

"I thank you very much for being here. We have

gone through a rigorous process with your selection in a very unique case. It is a death penalty case. We have spoken with each of you. We have determined that you are fair and just and will be fair and just in the judgment of this case and that is all that we ask."

Thomas Pope called as his first witness, Debbie Brisson, Terry's friend who tripped over Earl Robertson's dead body that November morning. She wore a navy-and-green plaid suit and white blouse, her curly reddish hair parted on the side and flowing to her shoulders.

"Did you know Terry and Earl Robertson?" Pope asked.

"Yes, I did," Brisson responded, slowly blinking her eyes.

"OK, could you tell us approximately how long or how you came to know them?"

"For about a year and a half, and I knew Terry from work," she said, looking toward the jury.

She explained they became good friends and talked on the phone every day if they didn't see each other. Pope asked her about the morning of her friend's death.

"Before Linda called me, I had also been trying to call Terry and realized her phone was off the hook because she had called me at home the previous night about eleven o'clock and left me a message. She had the telephone voice mail, so when it rings one time and it clicks over immediately to voice mail, you know they're either on the phone or the phone is off the hook, but I had called so many times that I had determined it was probably off the hook."

After Linda Weaver called and said she was concerned, Brisson went to the house.

"When I first got there, Terry's car was in the garage like normal. The van was parked on the side like normal and Earl's car was gone, so I just thought Terry had overslept."

"At that point, what door did you go to?"

"I always went to the carport," she said. But when Terry didn't come, she went to the basement door, which was underneath Terry's bedroom. The glass in the basement door was broken.

"I just went in the door and up the stairs," she said, pursing her lips.

Pope asked her what she observed when she got to the top of the steps.

She closed her eyes as she said, "Well, it was fairly dark as I was going up the steps because I didn't turn any lights on, just the daylight coming through the window. I opened the basement door. The basement door opens against the bathroom. It was still kind of dark and I rounded the corner to go toward Terry's bedroom."

"And what was your purpose going to Terry's bedroom?"

"To wake her up.

"When I opened the basement door and started to step forward, I stumbled onto something. I looked down; it was a male body laying there with just underwear on, laying facedown on the floor."

"Did you recognize the male at that time?"

"Um, I can't say that I actually recognized at that point. I guess I was just in shock that I'm not sure. I guess I assumed it was Earl."

Robertson wiped his eyes as Brisson testified.

Pope's next witness was Greg Maggart, the sheriff's deputy who responded to the scene after a call from

Earl Robertson's secretary. He explained a number of photographs showing the Robertsons' house and where he helped Brisson out of the house. James Robertson, sitting at the defense table in the room darkened so jurors could see the slides of the house, craned his neck to see the pictures. He looked like someone in a crowd straining to see a parade.

Maggart explained how he and Rollins walked through the house, clearing each room and then going up the stairs.

"At the top of the stairs, what, if anything, did you encounter?"

"I encountered a . . . body."

"Could you describe in detail what you observed?"

James Robertson looked on, expressionless, his cupped hand lightly resting on his mouth as Maggart described the scene.

"Uh, it appeared to be a male laying on his stomach; the only thing he had on was his underwear. Large amount of blood surrounding the body and it was on the walls and on the ceiling."

Pope asked what he did then. Maggart said he stepped over the body to see what was in the other parts of the house. Rollins stayed beside the body, watching Maggart's back. He told jurors he found another body in a back bedroom.

Robertson, his hand still resting on his face, averted his eyes and looked down slightly.

"It appeared to be a female, she was off the bed, some of the sheets were pulled off on top of her," Maggart explained. "There were several large lacerations and a lot of blood around her also."

Maggart said once he and Rollins were convinced no one was inside the house, they secured the scene.

The jury was taken from the courtroom as Ralph Misle took the stand. The judge wanted to hear what he was going to testify—before the jury did—to determine whether it would be admissible.

Pope asked about an interview Misle had with Robertson.

"I'll read from this follow-up, Mr. Pope: 'Subject Robertson was at York County Detention Center when he was interviewed by Lieutenant Hager and Detective Misle. Subject was advised of his rights and stated to officers that he would talk with us but there were certain aspects of the case that he would not discuss. We covered all aspects of his prior incarceration, habits in reference to his use of alcohol and drugs and the relationship with his parents. He stated to us that during his time in prison his mom would come to see him often and send him items via the mail system. These items would consist of writing pads and pens. He stated his mom would visit on a regular basis and their relationship was pretty good. He stated he and his father did not get along well but they seemed to have worked out a solution to their relationship. He stated that he was looking forward to moving in with his parents and that things were working out between them. He would not talk about the investigation except to say there were only two people who knew the truth about what went on in the house that morning and that was Meredith Moon and himself and the real truth would come out at the right time.'"

Also during the interview, Misle said he asked Robertson how the items came to be in the trash bin in Maryland. Robertson said he did not know what was in the trash bag or how it got into the car.

With the jury still out, Robertson took the stand. Under questioning from James Boyd, Robertson said he asked for an attorney in Philadelphia before Misle questioned him.

Pope asked who questioned him in Philadelphia. Robertson said he did not know.

Pope asked whether he was read his rights. He said he had been. Pope asked whether he answered any questions. Robertson said he told officers he would answer the questions he felt like answering, including where he came from.

"Did you answer any questions concerning this case?"

"Not that I remember. Basic stuff, my parents' names."

"Did you tell them anything about driving up to Philadelphia?" Pope asked, his arms crossed as he stood directly in front of Robertson.

"I might have. Not that I remember."

"Did you tell them anything about the Maryland Dumpster?"

"No, sir."

"Did you tell them anything about using the credit card at the Peach Stand?"

"I don't believe so," Robertson responded, shaking his head and looking up at Pope.

"Did you tell them that your parents were alive when you left the house?"

Robertson looked away, pursed his lips and raised his eyebrows before he answered: "Not sure."

Robertson told Pope he was questioned by at least

three homicide detectives, but he couldn't give any descriptions. He said he believed they were white.

Misle then took the stand as Judge Hayes considered whether to allow Robertson's statement. Hayes ultimately ruled that it could not.

Misle testified about the note that Robertson left on the kitchen table saying he was going to Philadelphia to pick up his brother, Chip. He said after talking to neighbors and checking records, he put out a nationwide alert for Robertson, Moon and the car and described the couple as "armed and dangerous." He contacted NationsBank and found the credit card was used just before nine in the morning. He also contacted the fugitive squad in Philadelphia, which arrested Robertson and Moon at 8:32 that evening.

Wayne Langley, a large man who lived across the street, described seeing Robertson and Moon that morning put something in the trunk of a red car.

"I slowed down to go into my driveway and I looked over there at them and Jimmy stood up—he was leaning into the car—and waved at me, and the young lady at the back stood up and turned around and waved also. I didn't know her at the time."

Langley said he went back into his house, read his Bible awhile and then left for work about an hour and a half later. When he left, the red car was gone. When he came home that afternoon, the street was full of police cars and newspaper reporters.

Pope built his case as any prosecutor does, step by step: police investigators, the coroner, photographs and clothing recovered from the Dumpster along Interstate 95 in Maryland. Maryland State Police trooper Guy Cox testified about finding the evidence in the trash bin at an Exxon station in the median on Interstate 95.

"After removing nine to ten items, I discovered a green trash bag with an aluminum bat handle sticking out of it," he said.

Chapter 17

On Friday, Meredith Moon took the stand. She wore a navy blue jail uniform and orange flip-flops. Her blond hair was cut above her shoulders and wispy bangs feathered across her forehead. She was visibly nervous, sitting forward in the chair, a timid look on her face. She glanced quickly at Robertson, sitting about ten feet away and wearing a gray suit, blue shirt and tie.

The television and still cameras of the ten news organizations represented in the courtroom intimidated her. She was also uncomfortable knowing she was about to talk about her drug use when her mother and father were sitting in the courtroom. She had been leading a double life and now had to confess it publicly.

"Can you tell me if you know the defendant, James Robertson?" Kevin Brackett began.

"Yes."

"How do you know him?"

"He dated my best friend, Erin."

"When did you first meet him?"

"About mid '95."

"Can you describe briefly for the jury how your

relationship with Mr. Robertson evolved from the time you met him till November 1997?"

"We partied together after work, hung out at his apartment. Mostly just hung out together."

She said they started working together in the fall of 1997 at the Pizza Hut in the food court at Winthrop University. She'd been working there since September.

Moon testified she picked Robertson up at his house on the morning of November 24, the day before the Robertsons were murdered. They drove to Rock and Roll Emporium in Charlotte and stayed there about an hour and a half shopping for candles and T-shirts.

When they returned to Rock Hill, she took him to work and she went to apply for a job at Village Pizza. Then she went home, where she stayed until she went to Outback Steakhouse to eat with a friend, Jeremy Martin.

Between 11:30 P.M. and midnight, Erin Savage picked her up at her house and they went to Erin's apartment; then, about an hour later, they headed to Robertson's in Erin's green S-10 pickup. Like Erin Savage, who testified earlier, she said they took a pool cue for Robertson to look at. In the thirty to forty-five minutes they were there, Moon snorted a couple of lines of crushed Ritalin, the drug given to calm children with attention deficit disorder. The drug has an opposite effect on people who do not need it. Robertson's parents were upstairs, but they did not see them. Robertson snorted a couple of lines of Ritalin as well.

Erin took Moon back to her apartment to pick up Moon's purse and then took her home. Moon spoke to her father for a few minutes and went upstairs to watch television. She couldn't sleep. The Ritalin made her feel antsy, hyper. At about 3:00 or 3:30 in the morning, Robertson called and asked if he could use a credit card belonging to Moon's mother to get a bus or plane ticket for his brother to come home for Thanksgiving. Moon refused. He called again around five o'clock. She still was not sleeping.

"Come over and bring traveling clothes," she recalled him saying.

Moon assumed they were going to Philadelphia to pick up Chip Robertson. She told her father she was taking Erin to the hospital to get treatment for a cut finger.

"I didn't want to tell him that I was going to Philadelphia with somebody he didn't know to pick up somebody he didn't know, so therefore I did lie to him," Moon testified.

She bought a pack of Marlboro Menthol Lights at the Circle K, drove to the Robertsons' and parked her blue Honda Accord on the street at the edge of the Robertsons' property.

He met her at the back door. He opened the door for her and they went inside and sat down. They talked for a few minutes. She looked at the coffee table and saw a note: "Trash bags. Need to scrub out the shower for blood."

"I'm going to do it," he said. "I'm going to kill my parents."

Robertson stared at her as she testified. She could feel his eyes on her, but she did not look at him. She knew he was trying to intimidate her. He wanted her to feel like she was betraying him. He still had power over her.

She testified she was not particularly surprised by his statement that he was going to kill his parents. He'd talked about killing his parents before. In fact, he'd talked about it many times before, for a year and a half. He talked about it while he was drunk, while he was sober. He wanted the insurance money, she said. But not until that night had he revealed a specific plan. He told her he was going to wait until his parents' alarm sounded and his dad got in the shower. He'd kill his mother first.

She said she tried to talk him out of it. He told her to put socks on her hands and pour the contents of one bottle of Tilex into another. She went in the bathroom and combined the bottles.

They crushed more Ritalin and snorted six to ten lines over the next two hours. It was his brother's prescription. He was a little more hyper than usual. He told her to go into his bedroom and sit on the couch. Robertson left, and she didn't know where he was. She heard the alarm go off.

"I heard some footsteps upstairs and then I heard the shower start running," Moon testified, her voice beginning to crack. "A couple minutes after the shower started running, I heard, like, signs of a struggle and I heard his mom scream. And she was screaming for Earl and she kept saying, 'No, Jimmy.'"

As she told of the mother's last words, Moon started to cry. She was hearing the screams in her head again, as she had many times before sitting in jail cells in Pennsylvania and South Carolina.

She testified the words were so piercing, so anguished, she put her hands over her ears. The screaming went on for about a minute. Moon went outside on the patio and smoked a cigarette. The family's pet rabbit was running around in circles in its cage, about eight feet to the left of the back door. After about a minute, Moon went back inside and sat on the couch in Robertson's bedroom.

Moon regained her composure as she continued her testimony.

From upstairs, Robertson said "Meredith" in a loud whisper.

She went upstairs and saw him at the end of the hallway covered in his mother's blood.

"He told me to get a knife from the kitchen," Moon said. "I tried to get out, but the door was locked. I got the knife, gave it to him, and he told me to go back downstairs."

The shower was still running.

"I heard a thumping noise," she said.

The shower had stopped.

"It was loud enough for me to hear it downstairs. It was like a hand beating a pillow."

"How long did that go on?" Brackett asked.

"I'd say about a minute."

"Could you hear any voices, any words?"

"No, sir."

"What happened after that?"

"After that, Jim came back downstairs and he started just walking around. I wasn't paying much attention to what he was doing. I was sitting on the couch in the bedroom. He had blood all over him, all over his clothes, his shirt and pants."

"Did you talk with him at all?" Brackett asked.

"Not that I remember," Moon answered, her voice level, without emotion.

"What did he or you do then?"

"Um, I went into the living room and then he was in the living room also and he thought he heard something upstairs. He told me to be quiet for a second. He thought he heard something upstairs and he went back upstairs."

"How long was he gone?"

"About five minutes."

When he came back, he was standing in the hallway, took off all his clothes and got into the shower. He was in the shower about five minutes and then he dressed. The bloody clothes were in a garbage bag in front of the fireplace in the living room.

It was about 7:45 A.M.

"He told me to get the bag and we went out the downstairs door. He picked up a rake and bashed the window in."

They walked up the hill to the driveway and Moon put the bag in the trunk of the red Mazda. They waved at a neighbor across the street. They got in the car and drove off.

Moon was driving. They went first to a BP station, but Robertson recognized someone there, so they went to the Peach Stand instead. They used Earl Robertson's credit card to buy gas, some Neosporin and Band-Aids.

"Jim cut his finger pretty badly busting out the window," she said.

Moon testified she called Erin and told her they were going to Philadelphia; she lied and said they were already halfway there.

As she testified, Robertson looked down at the floor.

During the ten-hour drive to Philadelphia, Robertson told her he had broken the knife blade off in his mother's neck.

"He kept saying, 'Chip's going to be so proud.' He said that over and over. He said he was glad it was over."

In the car, Robertson seemed buoyant. He sang to the radio. He talked about building a house on a lake with his inheritance; maybe he'd buy a club in Rock Hill and renovate it.

"Did he discuss with you what was supposed to happen next?" Brackett asked.

"He said that he was going to pick Chip up and we were going to drive back. He was going to let me out and I was to go home, and him and Chip were going to discover the bodies and call 911, et cetera."

When they arrived at Chip's apartment, no one came to the door. They walked around back and Robertson, agitated, knocked on the window. Still no answer. They left and ate dinner at Fiesta Pizza. She had chicken parmigiana. He ate a steak. She didn't remember whether they used Earl Robertson's credit card to pay for it or paid for it themselves.

About thirty minutes later, they returned to the apartment.

"We were on a one-way street. Jim was driving and trying to parallel park. Then I saw a car coming in the wrong direction. Two men came at us with guns. I was placed under arrest. Yanked out of the car by my hair, slammed on the pavement and put in the back of a car."

"Did Jim say anything to you?"

"No he did not."

Moon said she was taken to the Philadelphia Police Department and put in an interrogation room in homicide. In her first statement, she told investigators she was in the car when Robertson killed his parents. She was concerned about how the jury was reading her, whether they believed what she was saying. She tried to look at them as often as possible and to keep a check on her emotions.

"I was so nervous," she said later. "I was trying to appear less nervous so I'd appear more credible."

She told the court she changed her story the day after she was arrested. She told Rock Hill homicide detective Misle she was in the house when Robertson killed his parents.

"I did not tell them about going upstairs," she testified. "I didn't want to incriminate myself."

She told the jury she pleaded guilty the day before to two counts of accessory after the fact and armed robbery. She accepted a plea bargain, she said. The murder charges would be dropped if she testified truthfully in Robertson's trial.

"How much time are you looking at?" Brackett asked.

"A minimum of twenty, a maximum of sixty," she responded. Her voice broke and tears welled up in her eyes.

"Did you strike any blows in that house that night?"

"No, sir, I did not."

"Were you standing by watching as someone was killed?"

"No, sir, I was not."

"One final question, Meredith. You went outside to smoke a cigarette after his mother was murdered. And you're standing outside. Why didn't you run? Why didn't you run back to your car? Why didn't you run over to a neighbor's house?"

She looked briefly at the jury. She knew Brackett was going to ask the question, but in their rehearsals, he had told her not to answer. She didn't know until that moment what she would say. She didn't think. She spoke from her heart.

"This is the one question that's been hounding me for almost a year and a half. I was terrified. I was in shock. You've got to understand that during my relationship, friendship, whatever it was with Jim, he took advantage of me. He manipulated me and he played me. That made me more terrified of what would happen if I did run. It made me terrified if I didn't. I did not know what to do, so I did nothing. I was so scared, so I went along with whatever he did because that was the only thing that I knew to do."

"Did you go to that house with the intention of hurting anyone?"

"No, sir, I did not."

Bill Hancock rose to cross-examine Moon. Forcefully he hammered at her deal with the prosecution. He asked how many times she had been in the courtroom. She responded she was in there pleading guilty the day before and she was in the courtroom with the prosecution the week before practicing her testimony.

"So, you've been over and over this testimony, how many times?" Hancock asked.

"A couple."

"With the solicitor's office or whom?"

"Just once with the solicitor."

"Do you normally use the words or did you learn the words 'demeanor' and that sort of thing?"

She felt Hancock was trying to get to her, trying to insult her by insinuating she was not intelligent. His plan was to make the jury think she had been prompted by the solicitor, that she was too dumb to use such words. She started to get angry but held her emotions in check.

"I've always used them, sir."

"When you pled guilty yesterday . . . that was under agreement by the solicitor's office?"

"Yes, sir, it was."

"You knew you could have been charged with the death penalty and received death for your participation here, didn't you?"

"Yes, sir."

"And you knew you could either go to the electric chair or possibly receive life in prison without the possibility of parole, didn't you?"

"That was what I was facing, yes."

Brackett rose to object: "That's not a correct statement of law."

Hayes overruled the objection.

Hancock continued: "You knew that was a possibility. You pled guilty to armed robbery."

"Yes, sir."

Her anger surged again. She worried what the jury thought of her and he was trying to make it seem she had taken the easy way out, that she had pinned the murder on Robertson to save herself.

"Ms. Moon, let's go to the portion of your testimony. Now, as you sit here before us, you don't have the same appearance as you did in November of 1997."

"No, sir, I don't."

"You've lost approximately ninety pounds, haven't you?"

"About that, yes, sir."

"Now, how much did you weigh on November 25, 1997?"

"I'd say around two-seventy to two-eighty."

The question hurt her. Like most overweight people, Moon was self-conscious. She had been fat all her life, and now that she had lost nearly one hundred pounds, he was bringing up her size in front of a courtroom full of people and the tens of thousands who would watch on Court TV.

Years later, Moon said, "It wasn't the point that I had the ability to overpower Jim, that's what he was getting at. 'Well, you used to be one fat girl, huh?'"

Hancock continued: "I will also ask you to clarify some things for me. You say you got a phone call from Jimmy at five o'clock in the morning."

"Yes, sir, that is correct."

"And he asked you to come over."

"Yes, sir."

"And before that, you had been in Jimmy's apartment snorting Ritalin, is that correct?"

"Do you mean his parents' house? Yes, sir, we had."

"When you say a line of Ritalin—the way you do that is you crush it up and snort it through a straw. Is that correct?"

"It can be through a straw. It can be through a piece of paper."

"How much is a line?"

"I'm not sure. I've never crushed one up."

He asked how many times they used Ritalin. Was it a regular activity? She said it wasn't, that they had perhaps done it as many as four times. Hancock wanted to know whether it was the same sort of high as cocaine. Moon said she had never used cocaine, but then on subsequent questioning, she admitted she had used crack, a derivative of cocaine.

"What effect does Ritalin have on you?"

"It dulls my senses, my perceptions and awareness. It causes insomnia. It made me feel like I was sort of detached."

"It does give you those feelings and you take it for that reason, don't you?"

"Yes, sir."

"Do you suffer from any mental disorder, mental disease?"

She wanted to laugh but knew it was inappropriate. No one had ever asked her that.

"No, sir, I do not."

"Do you suffer from anything that would obscure your memory?"

"No, sir."

"Would the Ritalin obscure your memory?"

"I don't think so."

"But it's a drug, a powerful drug, so it could alter the way you look at things."

"That's a possibility, yes."

"That's why you take it."

"Yes."

He asked how many milligrams she or Robertson took that evening. She said she did not know. He also asked whether Robertson smelled as if he had been drinking. No, she said. Hancock wanted to know whether she made lying a habit. She said she did not.

"On this evening, just to start, you lied to your dad, did you not?"

"Yes, sir, but under the circumstances, I felt it was OK. I did not want my dad to think I was going up to

Philadelphia with a guy who he did not know, so I chose to tell a lie to him."

"You chose to tell a lie to your best friend, Erin, is that correct?"

"Yes, sir, that is correct."

"You had no trouble doing that evidently."

"Actually, I did. I do not lie to my best friend, but I did on that occasion."

She was ready for that question. She knew from the beginning how important it was to admit her own shortcomings and failings to build credibility with the jury.

"So you decided, since it was convenient, that you'd just go ahead and tell that lie. It was easier to tell a lie than it would have been to face the consequences."

"That is correct."

"Is that what you're doing now?"

"No, sir, it is not," she said, looking at Hancock.

"It's not?" he asked.

"Everything that I have said today I have also told my attorneys. I am not saying anything just because Mr. Pope or Mr. Brackett want me to. Everything that I have said today, and will say today, I have said to my attorneys before, many times."

She said she had testified to things that had incriminated her.

Moon's parents, Patty and Doug, sat together in the audience as their daughter testified. Patty Moon held her head down for most of her daughter's testimony. Moon didn't want to see her parents' faces and did not look for them in the courtroom, which was so full, people were standing along the walls. Moon tried to block it all out and concentrate on only the person questioning her and the jury.

Hancock asked about her false statement to Philadelphia police. Under his questioning, she admitted she said she had never said anything about Robertson wanting his parents' insurance before.

"When y'all are going up the road to Pennsylvania, you said that Jimmy said . . . Now, Chip's his brother, right? And Chip is the one you're going to see in Pennsylvania. Jimmy said, 'This would make Chip proud'?"

"These were his words exactly, because I remember it very well. 'Chip's going to be so proud.' He said that over and over."

James Robertson looked on dispassionately.

"Did that not strike you as strange?"

"Yes, it did."

"Did that not strike you as an irrational thought?"

"From talks that Jim had had with myself and others, no, it did not strike me as an irrational thought."

"That's rational that he would kill his parents so he could get the approval of his brother? And you're saying that's rational?"

"Not to me, maybe to him."

"So, what is rational to you may not be the same thing that is rational to him at that time."

"That's a possibility."

"In fact, it's bizarre, isn't it? It's weird."

"To some extent."

Hancock questioned Moon's testimony that she saw Robertson taking his father's credit card out of the wallet, throwing doubt on whether Robertson actually committed armed robbery. Under questioning, she admitted she did not know which hand he used to take the card from the wallet or what he did with it after he got it.

He asked whether she recognized a piece of paper labeled STATE EXHIBIT 25.

"No, sir, I do not."

"That is not a list that you recognize at all?"

"No, sir."

"Did you write that list?"

"No, sir."

"Did you write any list that evening?"

"I wrote something on a piece of paper. Yes."

"What was it?"

"It said, 'Alarm clock, wipe blood from downstairs doorknob and dispose of yard rake.'"

"Was that what you planned to do?"

"No, sir."

"Well, then, were you not using that list for a reminder?"

"Jim told me to write that on the list."

"Have you seen a copy of the list?"

"I don't think I've seen a copy of it."

"I don't remember you telling the solicitor that you sat down with Jimmy and wrote that list."

"I do not remember the time or place that I wrote that list."

"You don't remember time or place you wrote the list?" Hancock asked, incredulity in his voice.

"No, sir, I do not."

"Ma'am, I'm not going to browbeat you. I just want to ask one other question. You've written a list that you're supposed to clean up blood from Jimmy's parents and you're telling this jury you don't remember when or where you wrote this list."

"That is correct and it wasn't a list that I was supposed to do. It was a list that Jim was supposed to do."

"You remember that succinctly, don't you?"

"Yes, I do."

Brackett rose for redirect examination. He showed her state's exhibit 169, a picture of Moon, Robertson and four others taken about the time of the murders. It showed a much-heavier Moon. Brackett asked that it be admitted into evidence.

He also asked her about using Ritalin that night and whether it obscured her thinking.

"Did you know what was going on was wrong?"

"Yes, sir, I did."

"Were you scared?"

"Yes, sir, I was."

Brackett asked about Chip being proud of Robertson's killing his parents. Moon said Robertson had talked so much about killing his parents, she did not think it any stranger than his saying he was going out for beer.

He also showed Moon the sweater she was wearing that night, a large brown sweater with yellow, red and beige stripes. A stain of blood about the size of a quarter was all that was on it. The jury was left with two very visible images: virtually no blood on her clothes and she was at one time a very large girl.

Her testimony finally over, Moon had one more challenge. She had to walk right past James Robertson at the defense table as she left the courtroom. He stared at her. He smirked at her. She felt mocked. She glanced at him briefly, and when their eyes met, Meredith Moon stalked away faster. She believed he didn't care about anything happening there, not about her or her testimony, not about being on trial for his life.

Moon was led into the part of the building that housed the detention center, where she would wait until she was sentenced for her role in the crime.

Dr. Joel Sexton, a pathologist in Newberry, South Carolina, who did the autopsies, testified next. Sexton had been the first medical examiner in Charleston County, South Carolina. After a decade, he moved to Newberry to start Newberry Pathologists. He performed most of the autopsies involving murders in South Carolina.

Holding the knife sheathed in a plastic bag, Sexton said the stab wounds on Terry Robertson were consistent with being made by a knife of that kind. Earl Robertson had a blunt-force injury on his head consistent with that from the tines of a hammer and an incise wound on the back of the neck from a knife. He had four blunt-force injuries on the back that were made with a cylindrical object.

James Robertson looked on expressionlessly as Sexton handled the knife, hammer and bat. Robertson's left hand rested carelessly on his lips. He became agitated, however, when Pope put a picture on the screen showing the bloody knife on the bloodstained rose-colored sheets of Robertson's parents' bed.

Sexton also testified that some of the wounds were made after the Robertsons had died.

As that Friday afternoon wore on, the prosecution also called to the stand Brett Baker, an investigator from the State Law Enforcement Division who conducted DNA evidence of the blood found in the Robertson home. He showed any number of overhead slides detailing the blood analysis and whose blood was found. The testimony may have been clear to a microbiologist or geneticist, but for the folks of Rock Hill and probably the jury as well, it was tedious.

The bottom-line testimony from Baker was that Moon's blood was not found in the house.

Chapter 18

On Saturday morning, the prosecution was near-ing the end of its case. James Robertson came in wearing a navy blue suit, blue shirt and red tie and sat down as he had the previous days at the defense table. He glanced around the courtroom and had a look that caused people watching him to believe he was enjoying the attention. Many people in the au-dience judged him to be cocky, aloof, a demeanor that Boyd would say later was mistaken for anxiety. Boyd and Hancock had talked with Robertson about his demeanor. They knew it would hurt their chances with the jury.

"He didn't have the demeanor of someone who was real remorseful," Boyd said years later.

Boyd remembered the case of Sylvester Adams, his first death penalty case. Adams, who was executed by lethal injection in 1995, left no doubt he was a cold-blooded killer. Still, during his trial when his mother collapsed and fainted, Adams jumped up to help her. Boyd didn't see any such empathy in Robertson.

Many who knew Robertson well saw him as cocky and aloof. He gave the impression that the world re-volved around him, that he was smarter than everyone he knew and could do anything better than anyone else. Egotistical was not a strong enough adjective to describe him.

He seemed nonplussed as a DNA expert testified that Terry and Earl Robertson's blood had been found on the claw side of the hammer that had been pulled from the Maryland trash bin.

When the prosecution was finished, Judge Hayes, standing behind the bench elevated above the small courtroom, with his right arm folded across his chest and his left hand at his chin, said, "Mr. Robertson, have you made a decision as to whether you are going to testify or not?"

Standing behind the defense table with his attorneys to his right, Robertson said, "Yes, sir, Your Honor, I have made that decision."

"And that decision is?"

"I choose *not* to testify on my behalf," Robertson said, emphasizing the word "not."

"All right, and do you wish to make at the end a closing argument on your behalf?"

"No, Your Honor, I waive that right as well."

He asked if the defense had any witnesses. James Boyd said they did not, but he had a motion he wanted to make. He moved for a directed verdict on the grounds that the indictment charged Robertson with murdering "James and Terry Robertson."

"There has been no evidence presented that has identified the two people murdered as James and Terry Robertson," Boyd said.

Robertson looked at Hancock sitting and then whispered to Boyd, "Earl."

"I'm sorry, Earl Robertson. Not James Robertson. I'm sorry. I misspoke. When I said 'James,' I meant 'Earl.' No witnesses have testified that have identified the two bodies as Earl Robertson and Terry Robertson."

"The motion is denied," Hayes responded quickly. "I think there is evidence in the record in which the jury could conclude those were the two people whose deaths we are talking about."

Kevin Brackett gave the closing argument for the prosecution. He told the jury at the outset that he wanted to apologize for all the commotion of the trial, the shuffling of papers and the rummaging through paper bags looking for evidence.

"I'm sorry if it seems like we've been kind of tripping over our evidence here, because we have. The problem is we have so much of it that we can't hardly help but trip over it. We have so much evidence that it's understandable that you might be a little bit confused."

He told them it was his job at that point to help them make sense of what they'd seen. He said he couldn't make sense of what happened in the Robertson house. That was beyond his ability.

"When you add it all up, the sum you arrive at without any doubt, not a reasonable doubt, not a shadow of a doubt, is that this man right here," Brackett said, his voice rising as he walked over to within a foot of Robertson and pointing at him, "James Dejarnette Robertson, seated right here, on November 25, 1997, brutally murdered his mother and father, Terry and Earl Robertson."

Robertson sat stone-faced as Brackett spoke, his lips pursed, his eyes looking at nothing.

"His mother as she lay in her bed. His father as he walked out of the shower he had just taken."

Robertson looked down at the table and then re-captured the far-off look he had before.

"He left their battered bodies in the house and fled up the East Coast to Philadelphia. Margie Jordan knew something was very wrong when Earl didn't show up for work that day. Sissy George knew something was wrong when Terry didn't show up to pick up that coconut cake she had made. The friends, people that cared about them, became concerned and called the law."

He recounted the morning phone tree: Sissy called Linda Weaver, who called Debbie Brisson, who went to the house. She met Greg Maggart there, who was sent by Margie Jordan. Brackett showed a slide of the house and then the staircase Brisson had walked up.

"It was dark in there and she couldn't see the legs of Earl Robertson. She almost fell over them. She ran to the phone. The phone was not on the hook. Instead, she almost tripped over the telephone cord because the telephone was tucked under a cushion just past that lamp. She was the first one in the house. She was in there when that house was left as this man left it. He took that phone off the hook so his mother couldn't call for help. Nobody anywhere in the house could have called to get help."

As he narrated the story of that November morning, Brackett's voice had an edge of anger and enmity. From his voice, jurors could tell he was sickened by James Robertson and his acts.

"An hour after, an hour after Mr. and Mrs. Robertson were brutally beaten to death, they're in there laughing and talking. Nothing seemed out of the ordinary."

He asked the jury not to lose sight of what the trial was all about.

"It's about money," he said. "This case boils down to a dollar sign. This greedy little man couldn't wait for his parents to leave this earth. He couldn't wait for the money to come to him, so he took it. He took them."

Brackett reminded the jury that it was Meredith Moon who led police to the evidence that was in the courtroom. He acknowledged that she did not tell the whole truth at first, but within twenty-four hours the substance of the story she had told in the courtroom the day before was on a piece of paper in the hands of law enforcement.

As he showed a picture of a much-heavier Moon, Brackett said he didn't know what the defense would say about her, but based on their questions, they would most likely make an issue of her weight.

"That Meredith Moon right there," he said, pointing to the picture, "is not the same Meredith Moon you saw over here. This Meredith Moon is a lot wiser. She learned a lot of lessons since this photograph was taken. And she's going to have to pay, ladies and gentlemen. She'll pay to the tune of twenty to sixty years in prison for being an accessory to the greedy little man by the name of Jimmy Robertson."

He said she was not the one with the bat in her hand or the hammer in her hand.

"He was the one waiting for his daddy to finish showering. He was the one that hit his father, not just with this end but with this end," Brackett said, pointing to the tines.

Robertson continued to look on dispassionately.

Brackett then reviewed the physical evidence that proved Robertson was the murderer. In South

Carolina, there were the bodies, the wounds, the blood and the videotape of Robertson and Moon at the Peach Stand. The hammer and bat found in Maryland had the Robertsons' blood on them. The yellow pants Robertson was wearing had one parent's blood on the front, the other parent's on the back. Also in the bag of bloody clothes and weapons was Chip Robertson's bottle of Ritalin. Robertson had his father's credit card in his pocket when he was arrested and the receipt from the Peach Stand inside as well.

Moon's confession was what tied everything in the case together, Brackett said. Law enforcement got the bloody bag out of the trash. They learned of the trip up the East Coast.

"What would have happened if she hadn't confessed?" Brackett asked. "All of a sudden, this plan doesn't seem so bad. Looks like a break-in. I was up in Philadelphia. Meredith Moon was the key and everything she testified to was borne out by the physical evidence."

The brutal beatings endured by Terry and Earl Robertson left no doubt as to who did them.

"Just in case, just in case there's one of you sitting in the box that says, 'I'm still not convinced. Maybe there's room for doubt,' there's one little present that this man packed away in his little bag of tricks before he ran up the coast to Philadelphia. State's exhibit fifty-three: the gray T-shirt," Brackett said, taking it out of a paper bag and holding it up for the jury to see.

"What shirt did Mr. Robertson choose to wear when he butchered his parents? A T-shirt with his picture on it. A blood-soaked T-shirt with him out having a good time with a couple of his buddies.

"Ladies and gentlemen, they put chairs in the jury room so you can sit down and deliberate over the evidence, so you can have a place to sit comfortably and talk about the evidence that you've heard. I submit to you that in this case, you don't need to use those chairs. You go in there and take a vote. You don't need to see any of this. You know what happened. You know in your hearts this man's guilty. Don't you give him the satisfaction of five minutes thinking maybe you're out there wondering whether he's guilty. Don't you give him five minutes," Brackett said, his voice full of passion.

"You go back there, you take your vote and come back in here and tell this guilty murderer that you know he killed his parents. You tell him he's guilty and you don't give him five minutes' satisfaction. Ladies and gentlemen, we've carried our burden of proof. We've done our job. We ask you that you do yours. Hurry back to this courtroom and tell the world this man's a murderer. Thank you."

Brackett put his head down and walked back to the defense table.

Bill Hancock rose and walked toward the jury box, located on the far side of the room from where he sat at the defense table. He was holding a yellow legal pad.

"You've heard much of the evidence and I will start with some things I observed and some of the things that I listened to, and I'm not challenging the solicitor's argument but some of the things that were said. First, the entire case basically hinges on one Meredith Moon, if I heard the solicitor correctly. You know that she has lied; she lied all the way up and down the East Coast by omission. She lied to the police; then she decided she was going to tell the truth, but then she said there was money involved." He reminded the jury she was facing the death penalty. "She'll say anything because it's her skin, folks. I don't know what happened there, none of us will know what happened there, but we're depending on Meredith Moon."

One of the main charges in the case, he said, was armed robbery of one credit card. She could tell the details of Robertson taking the card out of his father's wallet, but she couldn't say which hand he held it in. She talked about the mother's pocketbook being by the pool table, but the crime scene pictures show it at the foot of his mother's bed.

"If she'll fabricate one, she'll fabricate all," Hancock said.

"If there's any doubt that she's telling the truth, you've got to give the doubt to Jimmy Robertson," Hancock said. "The law requires you—not asks of you, not requests of you—requires you as a jury that if you find in any portion, any element in any of these charges, any reasonable doubt, then you are required to put down 'not guilty.'"

Hancock referred to Brackett walking over to Robertson and saying it was all about money. The solicitor did not show, however, that the Robertson children knew anything about how much money their parents had.

"This is not a million-dollar house," Hancock said. "The state has to prove somewhere along the line that they knew how much was here to convince you that that is what was there or that he was thinking in that manner. That's proof. Don't speculate, because the law's going to tell you not to speculate."

Trying to push doubt into jurors' minds, Hancock

Earl Robertson graduated first in his class at Georgia Institute of Technology in Atlanta.
(Courtesy of York County Circuit Court)

Terry Dejarnette studied French and art at Agnes Scott College in Decatur, Georgia.
(Courtesy of York County Circuit Court)

Terry and Earl were married in August 1970.
(Courtesy of York County Circuit Court)

Earl Robertson worked in an executive position at Springs Industries, a textile manufacturer, while Terry took care of the house and children. *(Courtesy of York County Circuit Court)*

Chip Robertson's high school graduation. *(Courtesy of York County Circuit Court)*

The Robertsons lived comfortably in a subdivision outside Rock Hill, South Carolina. *(Author's photo)*

Meredith Moon and her mother, Patty Durand Moon.
(Courtesy of Meredith Moon)

Meredith moved to Rock Hill to live with her father, Douglas Moon, during her last years of high school.
(Courtesy of Meredith Moon)

Meredith Moon said she sat on the bed in Robertson's room while he killed his parents.
(Courtesy of York County Circuit Court)

Jimmy Robertson and his brother Chip made the downstairs into a two-bedroom apartment.
(Courtesy of York County Circuit Court)

Jimmy Robertson left a note on the kitchen table telling his parents he had gone to get his brother at school in Philadelphia.
(Courtesy of York County Circuit Court)

When Terry's friend Debbie Brisson arrived, she found the glass in the back door shattered.
(Courtesy of York County Circuit Court)

The attack on Earl Robertson was so vicious that his blood splattered the upstairs hallway. *(Courtesy of York County Circuit Court)*

The contents of Terry Robertson's pocketbook spilled onto the floor as she was murdered. *(Courtesy of York County Circuit Court)*

Earl Robertson's billfold was found on the floor of the bedroom. *(Courtesy of York County Circuit Court)*

A knife, its tip broken, was left on the bed by the murderer. (Courtesy of York County Circuit Court)

Meredith Moon's car was parked in front of the Robertsons' house. (Courtesy of York County Circuit Court)

A car registered to Earl Robertson was impounded in Pennsylvania.
(Courtesy of York County Circuit Court)

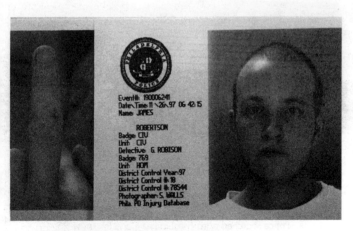

Jimmy Robertson's cut finger was photographed as evidence.
(Courtesy of York County Circuit Court)

Meredith Moon told police she and Robertson stopped
at a gas station in Maryland to throw out the murder weapon
and bloody clothes. *(Courtesy of York County Circuit Court)*

Police searched a trash container along Interstate 95
and found two of the murder weapons—a bat and hammer—
inside a black plastic bag. *(Courtesy of York County Circuit Court)*

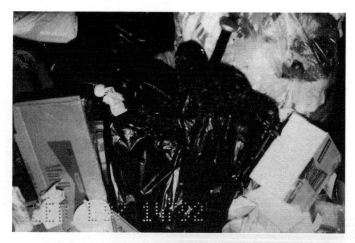

The baseball bat used to kill Earl Robertson was found in a trash bag in Maryland. *(Courtesy of York County Circuit Court)*

Police said bloody clothes, a hammer and prescriptions for Ritalin in the name of Earl Robertson, Jr., were found in the black plastic bag. *(Courtesy of York County Circuit Court)*

Jimmy Robertson was booked at the Moss Justice Center in Rock Hill, South Carolina, three months after the murders of his parents. *(Courtesy of York County Circuit Court)*

Kevin Brackett, deputy solicitor (left), and Tommy Pope, solicitor (right), prosecuted the case of the State of South Carolina v. Robertson. *(Author's photo)*

Bill Hancock (left) and Jim Boyd (seated) defended
Robertson (right) against murder charges.
(Courtesy of Andy Burriss, Copyright 1999 The Herald,
Rock Hill, South Carolina)

Robertson puts his
fingers in his ears as
the clerk of court reads
the jury's verdict.
*(Courtesy of Andy Burriss,
Copyright 1999*
The Herald, *Rock Hill,
South Carolina)*

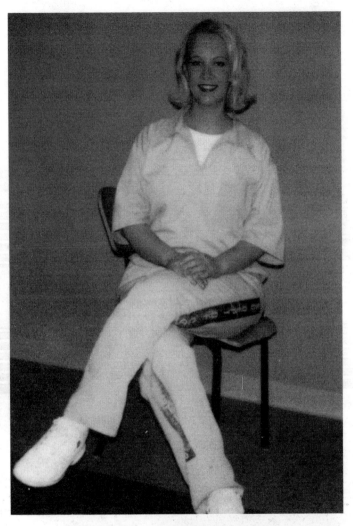

Meredith Moon is serving a 10-year sentence.
(Courtesy of Meredith Moon)

said the state's DNA expert said there was DNA in the house that was from other offspring. The state never told the jury how many children the Robertsons had, he said.

Boyd took over from Hancock after about twenty minutes.

"What has the state proved?" he asked. "The state has proved that Jimmy Robertson and Meredith Moon went to Philadelphia. The state has proven that a garbage bag connected to the murder of Earl and Terry Robertson was in a Dumpster in Maryland on that route and the DNA evidence that Terry's blood is on some items and Earl's blood is on some items. I want you to remember that Jimmy Robertson is not charged with accessory after the fact of a murder or disposing of evidence."

He said the only proof tying Robertson to the murder came from Moon. But Moon had shown she was a liar, he said. She admitted to four lies in court.

Boyd reached in a paper bag and pulled out a moccasin. The state cut a sample of blood from it, he said. It was tested for DNA.

"Remember what the expert said. It wasn't either of the murdered people. It wasn't Jimmy Robertson's blood. It was blood consistent with another child of the Robertsons'," he said. "It's evidence that somebody else was up there."

He said there was no testimony presented about Chip Robertson's whereabouts that evening.

"Has the state explained that to you? They have not and that's a huge hole in their case. If they can't explain that, go back to Meredith Moon's testimony— no matter how believable she is—if her testimony doesn't explain that, you can take it and throw it out the window. What did Mr. Brackett say? Without Meredith Moon, they don't have a case.

"Mr. Foreman, ladies and gentlemen, I ask you to carefully deliberate. Take what I've said. You can take it with a grain of salt, if you want to. I've tried to point out what I think is important in this case. Thank you."

Judge Hayes read the standard charge to the jury. He described the various charges that they would be considering. And he explained the concept of reasonable doubt. It does not mean, no doubt, he said, but doubt that any reasonable person would feel about the defendant's guilt.

The jury recessed to the jury room. Robertson was taken back to a holding cell. The temperature was in the mid 60s. Hancock went outside with a nine-iron for some practice shots. Boyd stayed in the courtroom and played with his two-year-old son. Brackett and Pope went back to their offices down the hall.

About two hours later, the foreman sent the judge a note handwritten on a piece of paper from a secretary's tablet: "The jury has reached a unanimous verdict." The word "unanimous" was written in above the line and in smaller print, as if an afterthought.

The parties reconvened in courtroom 1. It was March 20, 1999. If she had been alive, Terry Robertson would have been nine days from her fifty-first birthday. Sitting in his chair, Robertson wore the same stone face he had demonstrated throughout the trial. His jaw was clenched. He looked ahead at nothing in particular.

The clerk read the verdict:

"'*State of South Carolina* versus *James Dejarnette Robertson* under indictment number 98-GS-46-1020, the charge of murder, the verdict is guilty,' signed by the foreman. If this be your verdict, ladies and gentlemen, would you signify by raising your right hand, please?"

Robertson looked steely-eyed toward the jury.

"Let the record show that all twelve jurors affirmed this verdict."

The clerk continued reading. As she began to read the indictment for murdering his mother, Robertson raised his head up and closed his eyes. He grimaced. The temples in his head pulsed.

"'Guilty,'" the clerk read.

He did not look at the jury this time as his eyes welled with tears and his face turned red.

The clerk read the decision in the charge of armed robbery. Guilty. Financial transaction card fraud. Guilty. With every "guilty" read, Robertson had more and more trouble holding his emotions in check. At first, he tried not to cry. His lips quivered. He chewed on something in his mouth. He seemed on the verge of convulsions. Then he held his head up and sobbed. He rocked back and forth.

Robertson's attorneys knew from the start the prosecution had a strong case. They had long before decided against trying to mount an insanity defense, an almost insurmountable hurdle under South Carolina law. Only one woman in recent history had successfully waged that campaign, a woman who killed her son with a plumber's wrench as the family dressed for church. The guilty verdicts were expected by all involved and all watching.

James Robertson was the only one in the full courtroom who seemed surprised. No one reached to comfort him. The one woman who had always fulfilled that role was not there.

Chapter 19

South Carolina law requires a jury wait twenty-four hours before coming back to consider whether someone deserves to die for his crime. The jury that would decide whether James Robertson lived or died spent Sunday—their day off—at the Microtel Inn in Rock Hill, where they had been sequestered since Wednesday night, after the first day of testimony. Six agents of the State Law Enforcement Division stayed with them, ensuring they did not watch television reports of the trial or read about it in the newspapers.

The *Rock Hill Herald* and the *Charlotte Observer* both covered the proceeding extensively. That morning, the *Herald* turned much of its front page over to the verdict. The main headline was GUILTY: ROBERTSON CONVICTED OF MURDERING PARENTS. The story began with a vivid description of Robertson inhaling, rolling his eyes and sobbing when he learned the verdict. Also on the front page of the *Herald* was a story about the forty or so people who came to watch the trial out of curiosity and another relating an interview with Meredith Moon's mother in which she said justice was done. The *Observer* played the story on its metro front with a headline: MURDER VERDICT: GUILTY.

In South Carolina, murder becomes a capital

crime if more than one person is murdered, if the murdered person is a law enforcement officer or a child or if another violent crime is committed at the same time as the murder. The heinousness of the crime is considered an aggravating factor.

The punishment phase, Robertson's attorneys believed, offered them some hope for success. They believed they had a strong case with Robertson's history of mental problems and with the disorder and dysfunction they believed reigned in the Robertson household.

"The goal now is to save his life," Boyd told a reporter for the *Charlotte Observer* in its Sunday edition. He was counting on South Carolina's historical tendency of juries not giving death in cases involving family members.

Under South Carolina law, there are a number of circumstances juries must consider while weighing a death sentence. They are called mitigation. Among such circumstances are no prior violent crime, mental or emotional illness or mental retardation, the victim participated in the crime or consented to it, the defendant was an accomplice in a murder committed by another person and participation was relatively minor. Other mitigating circumstances are that the defendant was forced to act by someone else and the defendant's age when the crime was committed.

Boyd and Hancock felt confident about the evidence showing Robertson's mental illness: three years before his parents were murdered, James Robertson had been diagnosed as bipolar, an illness of incredibly high and low mood swings once known as manic depression.

On Monday morning, March 22, the prosecution began the penalty phase.

Kelly Bigham was called to the stand outside the presence of the jury to determine whether her testimony would be admitted. The prosecution wanted to show that Robertson was dangerous.

Brackett asked, "Do you know the defendant?"

"I don't know him. Yes and no. I've never met him or been introduced to him. He called me for a long time. He called me about the end of summer 1994 and said that he had seen me at a baccalaureate service a year before that and that I looked pretty in my navy blue dress. And I had a picture of me and my friend and I had on a navy blue dress. He said he was saving his money and he had a thousand dollars and he wanted me to have sex with him. And, you know, I told him no, but he kept calling."

Bigham said she was sixteen at the time and thought the caller was a friend playing a joke. The person called every night, late, on her private line in her bedroom. After he told her he was watching her and could see her in her bedroom, she realized it was not a joke.

"He knew what I wore to school," she said. "Who I sat with at lunch. That was when I was scared and I told my parents. The tracer was put on my phone and they called the police."

The calls stopped after about a week, she said.

"A few months later, I was in Sally's Beauty Supply and the woman said you have a phone call."

The caller, who was Robertson Bigham said, told her he wanted to take pictures of her wearing lingerie.

Hancock asked her if the person ever identified himself. No, she responded.

Christine Urmson, a bartender at the Silver Dollar bar in Rock Hill, where Robertson went in the fall of 1997, said Robertson would come in about 8:00 P.M. and stay until 3:00 in the morning. They would talk when there were few customers in the bar.

On a Thursday evening in October, she was talking to a customer and told him she was dating someone. Robertson was within earshot. That night, he turned uncharacteristically cold toward her. Ten minutes after he left, someone noticed her boss's tires were flat. When she left that night, two of her tires were flat.

The following Tuesday, she woke to a scraping noise outside her partially open window. It was dark. She saw a man's figure and jumped up and ran into the living room. She went to the front door and saw someone standing under the streetlight. It was Robertson's body type. She did not see his face. The next night, the same thing happened, but this time the screen was cut out. The next night, the same thing happened and she and a male friend who was staying with her opened the front door—Robertson was standing outside. They called the police.

Ann Catherine King went to school with Robertson from the seventh grade until the tenth grade at Catawba Christian School. For weeks, she received obscene calls, she told the judge. Her father put a trace on the phone, which showed the calls came from the Robertsons' house. She was working at the Body Firm, an aerobics business. She worked as a receptionist in the front of the building. Robertson came and parked his car and watched her for hours.

"I was uncomfortable. Many times, I called my father to come and follow me home," she said.

She called the police and the calls stopped.

Hayes ruled that the evidence was not germane and prohibited it from being admitted.

Brackett began his opening statement.

"Well, here we are. What a week ago was the unthinkable, the unbelievable, the incredible, that which we hoped wasn't true has been established by your verdict to be a fact that James D. Robertson did take the life of his parents.

"We've reconvened here because now we have to decide what are we going to do about this. What's the appropriate punishment for this crime? How should he be dealt with for what he did that early morning to his mother and his father?"

He said the prosecution would tell them more about Terry and Earl and about Robertson and the way he dealt with them.

"Long before he stole the credit card from his father, he had stolen so much more from them. Something so much more important. He stole from them the hopes and dreams that every parent has for their kids. The hopes and dreams that they're going to grow up better than you. They're going to have more opportunity. They're going to do more. They're going to be smarter. They're going to be better people. And every decent parent raises their kids toward that end."

He told the jury they would see pictures of the Robertsons' bodies so they could tell precisely what Robertson did to them. But he didn't just take their lives.

"He took their sanity," Brackett said, standing in front of the jury. "They were driven to the edge. The decision you're going to be asked to make at the end of this case, and is not an easy decision, and I assure you when Solicitor Pope gets up at the end of the presentation of all the evidence, no one will say this is a decision that should be made in five minutes.

"But ladies and gentlemen, I submit to you when you reflect on the evidence about who this man is and about what he has taken from all of us and how he did it, I submit to you, you will know, you will know what to do. You will know what's right in your head and in your heart, and you will leave this place changed, but you will leave this place knowing you did right and knowing that you did justice. Thank you."

Carrying a yellow legal pad, Hancock rose and strode over to the jury box.

"Ladies and gentlemen of the jury, we've been here together a week and now you have the most difficult decision before you that any citizen can have; and that is, are you going to put Jimmy Robertson to death?" he asked as he leaned on a podium at the edge of the jury box.

"Are you going to order the state to kill this twenty-four-year-old young man sitting here? No doubt in your mind that he committed the murders of his mother and his father. That's where we begin. That in itself is an unusual circumstance. It's not something you see every day on TV. It's not something you see anywhere. It's unusual. What brings us to the point where a child would kill their parents? It's weird. It's bizarre. That's where it is."

He said he agreed with the solicitor that everyone involved would be changed forever. They would be dealing with things they've probably never thought of before.

"To say that Jimmy Robertson is a troubled young

man doesn't even start. I'll go back to the testimony in the guilt phase. How troubled can you be when you ride up the road and say my brother would be proud of me? Is that something normal? Everyday? We're not in a soap opera here. We're in real life."

Hancock gave an idea of what was to come about the home life of the Robertsons, which he said most people considered a Beaver Cleaver existence.

"You're going to hear of mental illness. You're going to hear of histories of mental illness and mental illness in this family. It's not going to be pleasant. I don't revel going behind people's closed doors, but you never know what's there until you go behind those closed doors, and I'm going to eventually ask you to consider the mitigating circumstance that brought us to this point.

"A family that basically at the time that this happened was spiraling out of control to the point that the entire family was suicidal. That the mother had bipolar mental illness, not caused by Jimmy. Not caused by Jimmy. He can't cause bipolar mental illness. It's there."

Terry Robertson saw a counselor almost 200 times in three years. Earl Robertson was suicidal at the time also. Hancock told the jury they would hear evidence that James Robertson had bipolar mental illness. He was treated in a mental hospital.

"It becomes more than a job when you stand here and beg for a young man's life. We will all walk out of this changed. I just ask you to listen to our circumstances. I ask that you listen to the solicitor's circumstances. Evaluate them and then arrive at a verdict that speaks the truth. It's going to be one of two: death or life imprisonment. It's your decision."

The prosecution began with a series of people whose lives had brushed briefly against Robertson's. Lou Wylie, a teacher and guidance counselor at Catawba school when Robertson was a student and Earl was on the board of trustees, testified that Robertson was brilliant. He did well in his classes for the most part, but socially didn't have any close male friends. He sat at the lunch table with girls.

She remembered that Robertson had a confrontation with an English teacher and then demanded the woman be fired.

William Wood, the neighbor whom Robertson stole from, testified that he was at Myrtle Beach when he received a call from the Rock Hill Police Department. He left for home immediately and found all the drawers open and his belongings scattered all over the house. Among the missing were a car, three boxes of blank checkbooks, credit cards, a telephone answering machine, a television, a VCR and a lot of jewelry, some of it heirlooms from his mother and his wife's mother. In all, sixty-three items were missing, valued at $15,000. He found a battery charger sitting in the middle of the garage floor where the car had been.

"He had to charge the battery," Wood said.

Brackett asked if he recovered any of the stolen items.

"A damaged drill and electric typewriter and a little bit of costume jewelry," Wood said.

Robertson forged three checks to buy supplies at Texaco, roses for a girlfriend and a pair of shoes at Footlocker at the Galleria Mall. Wood's Sears credit cards were used to buy $9,000 worth of goods over two days, including several televisions, VCRs, tires and radar detectors.

Wood said Robertson broke in by taking a sharp object and punching a hole in a double-pane window just above the window lock. He reached in and released the window latch.

Brackett called Corrections Officer Michael Stobbe to talk about Robertson's behavior in prison. Reading from a printout from the South Carolina Department of Corrections computer inmate system, Stobbe said the first incident was in December 1996 when Robertson damaged property. Next was in February 1997, when Robertson was charged with fighting without a weapon. The same day, he had contraband, lied to an employee and damaged property. Robertson was sent to prison on September 3, 1996, and released July 31, 1997. He also had an infraction reported while he was in prison awaiting trial for his parents' murders. On September 17, 1998, he was written up for refusing to obey.

Hancock questioned the report, saying it appeared that Robertson was beat up and was not seen fighting back or with anyone.

"Yes, sir," Stobbe finally answered after repeated questioning.

Erin Savage, Robertson's ex-girlfriend and Moon's best friend, said Robertson was not close with his parents. He was usually angry with them. She met them only twice in the years she knew him. He was angry while they were dating because his mother had him arrested and taken to state hospital because she felt threatened by him.

"He was angry about that."

About a month before the murders, he was angry because his parents had cut off the brother. Five or six times, he told friends he intended to kill his parents.

"It would come up in everyday conversation, a couple of people sitting in a room hanging out," she said, brushing her long auburn hair, parted in the middle, away from her face. "Sometimes when he was drinking, sometimes when he wasn't. Usually when he was angry with his parents. He said he was going to kill them. Usually he wouldn't say why. Once he did say there was a lot of money involved. On one occasion, he said he'd make it look like a breaking and entering, and another occasion he said he'd burn down the house, but then he retracted that, saying he and his brother wanted to live in the house."

Brackett asked whether she had spoken with Robertson recently.

He called right before she came that morning and told her not to come because the case was running behind.

Boyd cross-examined Savage. Under his questioning, Savage said she was a good friend of Moon's, both before the murders and after.

"You introduced Meredith and Jimmy?"

"Yes, unfortunately."

She visited her in the detention center about once a month, but they did not discuss the case.

"Until the other day when I read it in the paper, I didn't know her full story of what happened that night," Savage said.

He also asked her whether Robertson used drugs when she was dating him. She said he did not. They didn't see each other often because her parents did not like him. Savage said she hung around with people who used drugs, but she quit using drugs two years earlier.

"You said you heard Jimmy talk about killing his

parents on a number of occasions," Boyd said. "Correct?"

"Yes, sir."

"Did you know his parents?"

"I met them a number of times. His mom, maybe three or four times. His father, twice."

"You knew where they lived?"

"Yes, sir."

"Did you ever go over to his parents and say, 'Hey, something's wrong here. Your son's talking about killing you'?"

"No, sir, I didn't. I wish I had. Every time Jim would say . . . I know I didn't believe he ever would. Jim is one of those people who talks a lot to get attention, and a lot of times, you don't listen or take at full face value what he's saying."

"You didn't take him seriously."

"I didn't take him seriously, sir."

"You didn't believe him. You thought he was just talking, right?"

"I mean, I could tell he wanted to, but I didn't think he would."

"Did you ever go to the police?"

"No, sir, I did not."

Justin Clayton Robinson, a beefy guy with a blond crew cut who described himself as Robertson's best friend, told the court he met Robertson when he worked at Mom's Country Store Restaurant. He said they were like brothers. He knew the family by being at the house regularly and knew his parents well.

"They weren't the type of people who you could sit around and talk about anything with. They were real serious about things. Like whenever I would speak with his dad, it was always what are you doing with your life? Do you plan on going to school? But I respected them a lot. They were good people."

He and Robertson went to clubs together, went out to meet girls and used drugs. One summer, they used a lot of crack, he said.

"Jim went to jail for that."

Robinson said he had been convicted of distribution of marijuana, but he no longer used drugs. He was attending York County Tech and wanted to go to Tennessee to school and ultimately go into business with his father as a cotton broker.

"Did Jim ever talk to you about his parents?" Brackett asked.

"On some occasions."

"Did he ever tell you how he felt about them?"

"Yes, he did."

"What did he say?"

"How he was a bad case of neglect. In a way, I could understand it, but, hey, this was what I was told. He flunked out of Georgia Tech despite his folks; they pressed school. It was a really big issue to Earl and they pretty much wrote him off as an alcoholic drug user and wouldn't—I wouldn't say didn't help him out but didn't help him out as much as before. They figured he was a done deal and they could start over with Chip, so they gave more attention to Chip."

"He resented that?"

"Yes, sir."

"Did he ever threaten his parents?"

"Not that I saw."

Robinson explained what that meant was that he had never seen Robertson threaten his parents, not that he had never *said* threatening things about them.

"He said he hated them and that he wished they

were dead. I remember him saying that he loved his mom. I know he loved his mom a lot more than he loved his dad."

Robinson looked down, occasionally looked at the jury and never looked at Robertson as he testified. It was clear he was pained to be telling a jury of the bad things his friend had said.

"Would you look at your statement and see what you told police when they questioned you along this same line back in 1997?" Brackett pressed.

"He had talked about killing them."

"OK, tell the jury about that."

"On a few occasions, he had mentioned some things about getting someone to do it or doing it himself. Of course, a lot of these times we were all under the influence of alcohol."

"Always under the influence?"

"Not always, not always."

"Did he tell you why?"

"I know that they were worth a lot of money."

"Did he tell you something about that?"

"He said he wanted their insurance money. His dad was planning to build a golf course or something after his dad retired, and he was afraid all the money would be spent and maybe they wouldn't get to inherit anything if they died naturally."

"Did he ever ask you to help him?"

"I know on one occasion he asked me if I would, you know, if he did it, if I would pick him up on the side of the road to help clear him, to give him some kind of alibi."

"How did he get along with his brother?"

"They were really close. I know that during that whole time period Chip had a pretty bad alcohol problem. Jim was worried about it; he was going to drink his life away."

"Did you ever see them get into any type of dispute?"

"On one occasion we were at the Oak's End, the motel, I think they tore it down. When Jim had first gotten out of hand and we were in the hotel room. I was working at Outback. We drank liquor all night and Chip got obnoxiously drunk, and I had this girl I was dating over there and Chip kept trying to hit on her. I brushed him off. Jim was, like, you need to sit down, you're being obnoxious, and they started fighting, and Chip got beat up pretty bad. He looked like a raccoon for a little while. Jim called Terry and said you better send dad over here before I kill Chip."

Earl arrived, wrestled Chip to the ground and took him home, Robinson said.

Under cross-examination by Boyd, Robinson told about their drug use. They smoked crack and marijuana and drank liquor. At the motel, Chip was snorting Ritalin; he and Robertson were not. They were all drinking liquor. Chip was making obscene comments. Jimmy got mad and called his parents. When Earl arrived, Chip hit him? Boyd asked.

Robinson responded Chip was swinging at Jim, and Earl got in the way.

Chip was the one who started misusing Ritalin.

"Were you friends with them at the time Jimmy committed the break-in at Mr. Wood's house?"

"Yes, sir."

"You pretty much know what went down. Chip was involved in that, wasn't he?"

"He wasn't involved with the break-in, but the break-in was made; items were stolen to trade to crack dealers to get crack cocaine and Chip participated in smoking the drugs that were gotten out of all that."

"Did he participate in disposing of or selling the stuff to get the money?"

"Yes, sir."

"Jimmy didn't say anything about Chip to the police? He took all the blame himself?"

"Yes, sir."

"Did you notice while you were friends with the Robertsons any change in Mrs. Robertson's physical appearance?"

"She was pretty large. She was very heavy. She continued to gain weight. She looked very unhappy all the time. Extremely unhappy."

He said he had never seen any physical confrontations between Robertson and his father but had seen them fight verbally.

"Basically, Earl trying to come down on Jim, basically telling him what a screwup he was."

"Did you remain friends with Chip after the murders were committed?"

"Yes, sir."

"Have you visited Chip in the home since Mr. and Mrs. Robertson died?"

"Yes, sir."

"So, you've remained friends?"

"Yes, sir."

"Did you go to the funeral?"

"I went to the wake at Bass Funeral Home."

"Was Chip partying? Did he throw a Christmas party?"

"He had a New Year's Eve party."

"The new year after his parents died?"

"Yes."

"Was there still some blood on the floor after that?"

"I believe there was a little bit on the wall and back in the bedroom."

"Wasn't Chip taking people around showing them?"

"Chip wasn't doing that. People wandered up there as the night grew older and people got drunker; maybe one person who had been up there an hour before would see somebody they hadn't seen and they'd say, 'Look upstairs, you've got to see this.' But Chip wasn't doing that."

Boyd asked where Chip was. In the F block of the detention center, Robinson responded. He was arrested for distributing cocaine and Xanax.

Scott Douglas, a former roommate, said even though James Robertson once asked him whether he had ever thought of killing someone to get their insurance money, he had not had negative feelings about his friend. Robertson was spoiled. His parents paid the bills, bought his groceries. His mother washed his clothes.

"I'd love to have it like that," Douglas said.

Darren Keller became roommates with James Robertson after he placed an ad in the newspaper. He needed to split expenses with someone. They drank beer together, shot pool. He met Earl Robertson when Jim Robertson moved in and again when he moved out, four days before the murders. Earl Robertson wrote the check for the deposit, Keller said.

Keller remembered an incident when James Robertson came home, grabbed a beer and asked whether Keller had ever been so mad at someone he wanted to kill them. Keller talked to him, encouraged him to continue doing well. Keller believed he calmed him. Robertson was talking about his parents.

But then a month or so later, Keller asked Robertson to leave because of the people Robertson was bringing around, mainly because they were using drugs, pot and Ritalin.

Stacey Peake, the fiancée of Robertson's neighbor Scott Langley, testified she went to the Robertson house one day in 1994. They got pizza and a movie. Scott, his sister, Beth, and Jimmy ate the pizza and then went back to the Langley house. They were watching television with him when a program came on about the Menendez murders, where two sons had killed their parents. At the commercial break, Robertson told her he and Chip planned to do the same to their parents.

"My face was a total shock," she testified.

Chapter 20

The autopsy pictures and the most gruesome crime-scene photos are not allowed as evidence during the guilt phase of the trial. They are considered prejudicial. But in the punishment phase, the rules are different. They are allowed. On Tuesday, Judge Hayes had a sign posted outside courtroom 1 warning spectators that "emotional and graphic" testimony and evidence were about to be heard and shown.

A State Law Enforcement Division videotape showed the path Debbie Brisson—and the deputies who followed her—took through the basement apartment and up the stairs on that November day.

"Oh, my God." One spectator gasped aloud at the gruesome sights of mutilated bodies captured on the ten-minute tape.

The tape showed an eight-inch gash on Earl Robertson's back and a deep gash on Terry Robertson's face, nearly covered by her blood-soaked hair.

Sexton, the forensic pathologist from Newberry, South Carolina, who completed the autopsies, took the stand again. He told the jury the details of the Robertson autopsies as Pope showed pictures on an overhead projector.

"You can see a pair of tine marks on her head," he

began as he detailed the injuries. He showed the deep lacerations on Terry Robertson's head inflicted by a hammer. Two other injuries were inflicted with the other side of the hammer. All of the injuries were inflicted before Terry Robertson died.

Robertson put his head down and did not look at the pictures.

Sexton showed the knife marks that were inflicted on Terry's face and neck after she died. He showed the wounds on her arms and back, all made after the heart had stopped and all superficial.

Robertson held his hand over his eyes.

The autopsy photos showed Robertson slit his mother's throat, a deep gash from her ear to her mouth. He cut large chunks of muscle and flesh from her forearms near the wrist and slit one arm so deeply the inside tissue folded over like a cabbage leaf. He stabbed her in the upper chest.

Earl Robertson did not die instantaneously, Sexton said, and the wounds were painful. The cause of death was injury to the brain. It could have taken a matter of minutes to die or longer. There was no way to tell.

When Hancock began his cross-examination and the lights came back on, Robertson raised his head. His face like stone, his lips pursed. Hancock asked about the fatal blows to the head.

Sexton said it would take adult force to inflict the fatal blow, not necessarily brute force, because of the way a hammer can be swung. It probably caused immediate unconsciousness, but Sexton said he did not know which of the injuries was inflicted first.

Sissy George said she learned of the deaths when Linda and Bill Weaver walked into her office at

Springs. She could tell by the look on their faces that something terrible had happened. They told her also that the police were looking for Jimmy Robertson. She and Linda drove over to the Robertson house in George's car to see what was happening.

The property was already taped off.

"Nobody but the camera people wanted to say anything, so I just got in my car and left," she said.

George said she and the Weavers did most of the funeral arrangements. She counted herself among the Robertsons' closest friends.

"Sissy, I want you to tell this jury what the loss of Terry and Earl through this crime has meant to you and your family."

"It was like losing a member of my family," she said, her voice shaking. "I had known her for thirty-three years. She had been there for me and I had been there for her. We shared the joys of our lives and the sorrows. I don't think it could have been any worse if my sister had died when this happened."

James Robertson wiped his eyes with a handkerchief.

On cross-examination, Hancock asked whether George considered Terry an honest person.

"Yes, I would."

"So, you feel like she told you the truth when she talked and had discussions with you."

"Yes."

"She discussed with you Earl's violent temper and that she was scared of him, didn't she?"

"Never," George said emphatically.

"She never did. She discussed with you that she thought she was promiscuous sexually in high school, didn't she?"

"Never."

"She discussed with you the fact . . ." His questions were rapid-fire.

Pope interjected: "Your Honor, I will object unless there is a basis for these questions."

"I sustain your objection," Hayes said.

"You think you knew everything about her, don't you?" Hancock said.

"I don't think you know everything about anybody," she responded in kind.

"You were aware that she was bipolar and had mental illness."

"I knew she had been diagnosed bipolar."

Robertson looked on eagerly and bit his fingernail. His composure returned.

"You knew she was seeing a counselor," Hancock demanded.

"That's correct."

"You're making a basic medical assumption. . . . You told the jury that she showed no tendencies toward that depression or mental disorder until when?"

Robertson looked back at someone in the audience.

"Around 1992."

"In 1992. Did she, in any way, ever discuss these mental problems with you?"

"No," George responded.

"Did she discuss her relationship with Earl?"

"I'm not sure what you mean by that question," George said, looking at Hancock.

"Any problems in that relationship, anything that had developed."

"No."

"She didn't?"

"No."

"You're assuming there were no problems?"

"I know of none that . . . She never discussed anything in specifics."

Earl Robertson's secretary, Margie Jordan, who had known him since 1983, took the stand next.

"How was Earl when you went back to work with him? Was he the same old Earl that you knew from three years before?"

"No, sir. He wasn't quite the same person. He wasn't quite as outgoing. He was friendly and nice to me, but he stayed in his office a lot like he was retreating to his office. He didn't have as much spunk and kid about him as he used to have."

Jordan said she learned her boss was dead from Miller Deaton, who was Earl's supervisor. Someone from the sheriff's office had called Springs to tell them.

"Margie, I want you to tell this jury in your own words how has Earl's death affected you?"

"Well, like I said, I was a close friend of Mr. Robertson for a long time. He was a great guy. He was a great guy to work for. One of the hardest things I had to do was clean out his office," she said as she started to cry.

She said she fussed at him for having no pictures on the wall when she first went to work for him. Finally he brought in a picture of a ship. She teased him. It belonged in a fish camp, she said. They put it on the wall and each time they moved offices—four times in all—she put that ship picture back up.

"When we cleaned out the office and packed his stuff up, I couldn't take that ship off that wall. One of the other managers had to take it down. I couldn't, knowing I wouldn't be putting it back up."

They wanted her to change the message on his voice mail. It took her days to do it.

"It was hard taking his voice off that phone. Every day, I get mail."

Jordan cried openly.

James Robertson did, too.

Jordan said Earl Robertson liked to tease her about her age because she was a few years older than he.

"He'd say he didn't know if he wanted to be seen with an old woman like me," Jordan said. "I was looking forward to his fiftieth birthday so I could get even with him, but it never happened."

Linda Weaver, one of Terry's best friends who had tried unsuccessfully to get the judge to grant her family status so she would not have to stay outside the courtroom for most of the trial, testified that her friend was the kind of mother who was always a room mother for her sons' classes.

"No matter if she had two children in school, she was room mother for the first and second grade of whatever grade they happened to be in. She was the mother who took the Kool-Aid and cookies to the baseball game. She was the mother who went to every PTO meeting. Or she was on the board at Catawba; when they were there, she volunteered at the school to help out at the office. She was always there."

Terry loved holidays.

Earl, too, was involved, although he worked during the day. He was involved with Scouts. He was at every game.

Six to eight friends went out to eat, celebrated Christmas together and exchanged gifts. They gave birthday presents to each other's children.

"Terry was as much of an aunt to my children. We

were each other's families. We were like brothers and sisters."

"How would you best describe Terry?" Pope asked.

"Terry was a loving, compassionate person. She . . . Terry was never too busy for anybody. If you had a problem, she would be there for you," Weaver said, her eyes filling with tears behind her glasses. Her carefully coiffed gray hair shone in the courtroom fluorescence.

Terry sat up with her for three days and nights at the hospital when her mother was sick.

"She was always there for you."

Weaver told the jury Terry wrote to her son every day when he was in Germany as a high-school student. When Earl told her the phone bill was too high from her calling overseas, she and Weaver would go to the gas station with a pocketful of coins to call him from a pay phone.

"Did there come a time that you saw a change in Terry?"

"Yes, sir."

"Can you relate to the jury when that was?"

"It was about the middle of the year when Jimmy was at Georgia Tech."

"Can you relate to the jury what change you saw in Terry?"

"I'm not saying we did not talk every day, but Terry would not discuss things that went on. Terry didn't talk as much. She didn't discuss her family. We couldn't go eat at certain restaurants because she was embarrassed. She wouldn't go to the grocery store because she was embarrassed. On occasion, she would actually look down the aisle to see who was coming because she was embarrassed."

"Embarrassed about what?" Pope asked.

"Embarrassed about the things that her son had done that other people knew about," Weaver said.

Weaver said on the day the Robertsons were murdered, Debbie Brisson called her and told her she had been in the house and found a body. She didn't know who it was but asked Weaver to come to Carolina Counseling, where Brisson worked. Weaver drove the twelve miles from her Fort Mill home. Weaver then went to the Robertsons and talked to the police.

"I probably badgered the police to tell me what was going on."

She knew something bad had happened, but they wouldn't say.

"I then told them that if there were two bodies in that house, they should be looking for their son."

"Did you tell them who the two people would be?"

"Yes."

Weaver said her husband flew on a Springs corporate airplane to Georgia to get Earl Robertson's mother. They found a place for her to stay and for Chip to stay. They helped plan the funerals. They wrote a eulogy.

"I went to the florist in Fort Mill," she said as she dissolved into tears, "and picked out two casket sprays. We then had a visitation at the funeral home, a funeral at the church. That afternoon, we drove to Milledgeville, and the next day, we had a funeral."

"In your own words, tell the jury what this man's actions did to you."

She sighed. "Well, I still go to the telephone to dial the phone number. I told Terry most everything. I don't have that person to tell anymore. When my son got engaged," she said, tears flowing freely down her face and sobs halting her words, "I went to the telephone to call her. When my son got married, she was supposed to be there. Even my son said Terry won't be there for you. Terry was my best friend. I'm not saying I don't have a best friend anymore. I don't have a friend like Terry anymore. I don't have somebody who I could call in the middle of the night if I needed them."

On cross-examination, Hancock asked whether Weaver knew that Terry had marital problems.

"I don't think Terry had any marital problems," she said.

"You knew she was receiving counseling from a psychiatrist and family counselor?"

"Yes."

"Terry's not the kind of person who would lie to one of those people, is she?"

"To the best of my knowledge. No, Terry did not lie."

"You could depend on what she said, is that correct?"

"Yes."

"Did she have any problems with the death of her parents?"

"Yes, we all have problems when our parents die."

"How long did those problems persist?"

"I really don't know how long it took her to get over it. My mother's been dead two years. I haven't gotten over that yet," Weaver said forcefully, staring at the defense attorney.

Brett Baker, a crime scene investigator for the State Law Enforcement Division, was called to the stand to describe the crime scene photos. He showed the blood spatters on the wall; most were eighteen to twenty-four inches from the floor, although some were at eye level. That meant at some point Earl Robertson was hit while he was standing, but most of the hits he took were while lying on the floor.

James Robertson turned his head away from the photos, which were displayed on a large screen for the jury to see, and held his hand over the side of his face. He then turned his face forward and shut his eyes.

"You look and see this type of mutilation, you think of anger," Baker said. "A lot of anger."

Robertson turned around and looked at someone in the audience. He seemed composed.

Hancock asked, "Agent Baker, you said that when you looked at those pictures, it showed you there was anger there, right?"

"Yes, sir."

"A great deal of anger?"

"Several things it can indicate. It could be anger. It could be various other mental conditions. It's an indicator, something that helped us know what we were looking for."

"In your experience, it shows rage. That scene shows rage," Hancock said.

"Several things in the scene shows anger; however, the totality of the scene also demonstrated things to be very methodical."

"It shows rage."

"Yes, sir, it shows anger."

"Like a person out of control."

"Again, I don't use the word out of control because of the fact that we had fabric impressions linked to socks. It was very methodical."

"You're saying someone planned to do it because they had socks on their hands."

"Partially, yes, sir."

"The amount of damage done," Hancock pressed, "the manner in which it's done. Doesn't it show a rage that is out of control?"

"It shows hostility and hatred," Baker said.

The prosecution rested its case.

The defense unleashed its opening barrage of testimony about mental illness with Dr. Ronald Prier, a psychiatrist at William S. Hall Psychiatric Institute, a state mental hospital where Robertson was committed by his mother in August 1995. Prier was his attending physician. He was civilly committed, which meant he was involuntarily hospitalized through an order from the probate court because he posed a danger to his mother. He was there from August 24 until August 31. Prier said he diagnosed bipolar disorder, mania and alcohol dependence. Robertson also had a urinary tract infection and an abnormal electrocardiogram.

He said bipolar disorder is a cyclic-mood disorder, characterized by mood swings, impulsive behavior, insomnia, racing thoughts or speaking. Typically, people in a manic condition do things they would not normally do, such as spending large sums of money or becoming promiscuous. Prier said the disorder has a genetic tendency and can occur from the teenage years until middle age. It's a lifelong condition that must be treated with medication.

During the hospital stay, Prier saw little indication of the disorder in Robertson, but family members and local counselors told of a clear history of a cyclic-mood problem. Robertson was treated with Lithium in 1994. He and his mother reported expansive moods, feeling abnormally confident. Robertson believed he could do things that were beyond what experience would show he could do. He reported he slept only thirty minutes a day.

He had three arrests for drinking while driving in the three months before he was hospitalized, Prier said, and he had had legal problems while an exchange student in Germany.

Prier said a condition like bipolarity is stressful in itself. He also found family strife.

"His family was understandably concerned about his potential to hurt somebody," Prier testified.

Prier arranged a family meeting while James Robertson was hospitalized, and it was clear, he said, that the family was under serious stress.

He gave him a prescription for Depakote, an anti-seizure medication found to be helpful in moderating mood swings, and Robertson was released.

Brackett cross-examined Prier. He asked about the Lithium prescription.

"You made it sound like the doctor took him off. Isn't it true [Robertson] felt the Lithium therapy was not effective and therefore he stopped taking it?"

"Correct."

"It cannot be cured."

"Definitely."

"It can be treated. In fact, there are thousands and thousands of people out there functioning right now with bipolar."

"Correct."

"They take medicine. It's under control."

"Correct."

"It doesn't cause them problems."

"There are people who do not respond to treatment."

"OK, certainly if they do not take their medicine, they are not going to respond to treatment. There's no chance they are going to respond to treatment."

"Correct."

Prier also said alcohol use aggravates the disorder. Under questioning from Brackett, Prier said he advised Robertson to stay away from alcohol and drugs, that he should take his medication and go to the Keystone Center in Rock Hill for counseling.

"All of your advice is for naught, if he doesn't take it," Brackett said.

"Correct."

At the family meeting, the parents expressed a great deal of anger about Robertson's past behavior and told the doctor that Robertson was causing a strain on family finances.

"The stress goes both ways," Prier said. "Typically, the parents, of course, are doing the best they can and they are also stressing the child and the child stresses the family."

"OK, but he was twenty-one years old," Brackett said. "He wasn't really a child anymore, was he?"

"Children still stress their parents, no matter what age they are," Prier responded.

"Their children, but he's an adult. He's twenty-one years old and they're still there trying to take care of him," Brackett said, "trying to help him out."

"The stress goes both ways," Prier said again.

"Yes, sir, I understand, because they love him."

"Of course."

"And they want him to do well."

"Right."

Chapter 21

On Wednesday morning, the defense jumped into the meat of its case: to try to show why James Robertson committed the unthinkable. They said they did not want to try to excuse his actions, but in some way to explain them.

Dr. Jonathan Pincus was a Washington, D.C., neurologist who had researched the lives of more than one hundred murderers and found most had brain injury, mental illness and a history of having been abused. He told the jury about a number of tests he did on Robertson. He was trying to determine whether Robertson had a brain injury. He found Robertson's frontal lobes were not working properly.

"Here is a guy who did something that he had been thinking about for a while," Pincus testified. "In other words, we know that there was an urge that he had to kill his parents. In fact, he was admitted to the Hall Institute in 1995 because of suicidal ideation and because of homicidal ideation that was directed at his mother."

Hancock asked whether Pincus found Robertson had suicidal or homicidal tendencies.

"Most of us have homicidal thoughts from time to time. 'This clerk in the supermarket, I can't stand them,' or somebody does something really annoying [and] you say, 'Ooh, I'd like to get them.' But you don't.

"Robertson had been having the thoughts for a while; the question is why on the night of the murder it becomes an action, not a thought," Pincus said.

Ritalin is a benign drug taken in low doses twice a day, he said. It increases the ability of people with frontal-lobe disease to pay attention. People who are sleepy can benefit as can people who are overweight.

Robertson was never prescribed Ritalin, and his brother, who was, probably was misdiagnosed, Pincus said.

"I don't know how this happened because I can't put down a prescription for more than a month," Pincus said. "They were able to get boxes of it. Brother was selling it and abusing it himself. Robertson was using it to self-medicate. To do something energetic he'd take Ritalin."

On the night of the murder, he took ten times the amount of a normal prescription. Pincus testified that the benefit of snorting it is that it works faster—five minutes compared with thirty minutes if taken by mouth. The bloodstream absorbs it faster.

"You get a higher blood level more quickly," Pincus said.

"What was his condition per your evaluation on November 25, 1997?"

"I believe at that time he had . . . I think the same dysfunctions I found on my evaluation in November last year were there then, too, because nothing happened in between that would cause brain damage that I know of. The history of bipolar illness didn't depend on my evaluation. It was made years before. He even went to Hall then. He was supposed to be on Lithium and it's used for one thing only, and that's treating bipolar."

Pincus testified Robertson was having an episode of mania at the time of the murders. He had three hours of sleep in the twenty-four to thirty-six hours before with a history of gambling, drug use, running up debts, not being able to concentrate.

Twenty percent of people with bipolar are obsessive-compulsive, Pincus said.

"He'd count fuzz balls off a couch. Books on a shelf. Spots on a wall. The number of times a pattern crosses in wallpaper."

Obsessive-compulsive disorder also shuts down a person's capacity to concentrate.

"The combination of the urge that he had been controlling up until that time to kill his parents, under the influence of mania and the drug Ritalin, which exacerbates the symptoms of mania reproduced then [and] accentuates them, that is the reason he did that. I also base that on what he did. This was no assassination. He obliterated them. He was gripped by a colossal emotion which was not cool assassination. His father's head looked like a tomato that had been burst by repeated beating. His mother, the same on one side. It was horrible. Stabbing in addition. His was no assassin's bullet."

"What could that colossal emotion be?"

"Well, it was an impulse, an urge, that was not only stimulated by the drugs he was on and the mania that he was having, but also not checked by the functioning of his frontal lobe, which was not working because of the medication he was taking and the alcohol he drank. The disease, the drugs, the damage, he already had."

"How would you explain the fact that he may have written a note saying he was going to do certain things as if he was planning it?" Hancock asked.

"I don't think that is the standard of determining whether he was out of control at the time he did what he did. What he did after, in other words. He may actually have thought of what he was going to do beforehand."

He said the covering up was not an effective plan and that it did not invalidate anything he said.

"Would it change your opinion if the notes were written before the crime or after the crime?"

"Depends on how much before the crime. There would be some presumption of planning, but the assassination itself—that's the focus and he was out of control."

Brackett began his cross-examination.

"There is nothing in here at all about antisocial personality disorder, is there?"

"Yes, there is a lot in here about antisocial acts. . . ."

"Maybe you misunderstood . . ."

The judge threw up his hands in disgust and reprimanded Bracket: "Let him answer the question, please, Mr. Brackett."

"He's not answering the question."

"I did not use the phrase 'antisocial personality' anywhere in my report nor did I use the words 'antisocial act.'"

"Thank you very much. On the same page further down, he indicated his relationship with his father diminished after he quit college. His father cut him off, in the sense he had to pay for his own health insurance and his own clothes, even though he was allowed to live at home."

"Yes."

"He indicated that his brother had an alcohol problem as well."

"Yes."

"And his father wanted him to go to Alcoholics Anonymous to get treatment for that?"

"Yes," Pincus said, looking down at the report he was holding in his hands.

"On the night of the murders, he indicated he took thirty milligrams of Ritalin to give him energy to clean the house."

"Yes."

"His plan was to have a few beers to come off the Ritalin to go to sleep."

"Yes."

"He was kind of like deciding what medications he should take and what order?"

"Absolutely."

"It was clear from your evaluation of the William S. Hall reports of 1995 that he had been told the effects of alcohol and drugs on bipolar."

"Yes."

"Down at the bottom of the page there, where he starts talking about the killing itself, he said the act was impulsive and not premeditated."

"Yes."

"Then he says he thought he could do this and get away with it."

"Yes."

"Then he says in the very next sentence, he didn't know if it was right or wrong."

"Right."

"If somebody doesn't know the difference between right or wrong, are they generally concerned about getting away with it?" Brackett asked.

"Well, the question of getting away with it means there's going to be a consequence to them of it. That's really a little bit different from thinking it was right or wrong. To think that something is right or wrong means you have kind of an emotional feeling about not doing . . . Everybody wants to do what's right and not do what's wrong. Part of the thing that keeps us from doing things that are wrong is that not only will we be punished, but even if we could get away with it, we would know it was wrong. We would feel that it's wrong. Those two things seem like an oxymoron, but it isn't. A person could do some criminal behavior, even outrageous behavior, and gets away with it and do it just because he could get away with it. Cheating on income tax. That's a relative frequent thing that people do."

Brackett asked about the last line of Pincus's report that said the only time Robertson thought of killing his parents was when he was taking Ritalin, cocaine or speed. That's an important part of the diagnosis? Brackett asked.

Pincus said it was not.

"The fact is, he did have thoughts of killing his parents when he was sober, but he didn't enact them. The difference between thinking something and doing something is very major. The times he would consider doing that, he was under the influence."

Brackett asked about the tests Pincus conducted on Robertson, including an eye test that could indicate a frontal-lobe dysfunction.

"If I was trying to hit a man in the head with this

baseball bat and he was ducking and weaving and dodging and trying to avoid being hit in the head, yet I was able to strike him in the head, that would seem to indicate that somebody's eyes were functioning just fine, wouldn't it?"

"No."

"No?"

"No. You could be blind in one eye and do that. You could be blind completely and do that. You could have frontal-lobe dysfunction and do that. The person I told you about—the doctor with a brain tumor—could drive a car even though he had frontal-lobe dysfunction, but he drove into barriers."

Brackett asked how much he was paid.

Pincus told him $4,000 and that he had been paid for the evaluation, not for testimony.

"Is neurology such a specialty that there are only a few?" Brackett asked.

Pincus said no, there were thousands, but they specialize in different areas. He was one of the few who had seen a large number of violent people.

Brackett asked about other trials in which he had testified.

He responded he had been involved in seventy-five to one hundred cases in twenty years.

Brackett sat down and Hancock rose for redirect.

He asked whether Robertson had told Pincus about abuse.

Pincus, reading from his report, said Robertson's father backhanded him in the car, punched him in the chest and beat him about once a week from ages five to fifteen. His father had a bad temper and threw him down the stairs and against a wall. His mother would intervene.

Pincus said Robertson reported a number of symptoms that would indicate abuse, including bed-wetting until the age of twelve. Robertson also had scars on his back that could have been from beatings.

Dr. James Evans, a psychologist, was called to the stand to testify about his evaluation of Robertson in September 1998, nearly a year after the murders. He spent six hours with him and read two psychological reports from four doctors and the social background prepared by Dr. Toni Cascio, a University of South Carolina social worker.

One test he performed showed Robertson had an intelligence quotient of 112. On verbal section, he scored 118, above average, and 102, average, on nonverbal. People with that much of a discrepancy between the two could mean they have brain dysfunction.

It showed the right side of Robertson's brain was not functioning as efficiently as the left side, Evans said. He pointed to an answer to a question about the similarity between poems and statues. Robertson responded that a poem goes up and down and a statue stands up and down. He should have said they were both works of art, Evans said.

"What were your conclusions?"

"As a result of the interview and the testing, I concluded that the earlier diagnosis of ADD has a physiological correlate to it," he said.

Robertson suffered from mania and had dysfunction of the right hemisphere and frontal lobe.

"This would likely be biological cause of having trouble with emotional control. Sometimes extreme, which I've seen in many other persons who have committed serious crime."

Evans said Robertson also said he experienced episodes of disassociation, where he did not think the world was real.

Brackett asked whether Evans was retained by the defense.

"Yes."

"When he told you on the first page of your report he had out-of-body type experiences where he seemed to be watching himself engaging in various behaviors. . . ."

"Yes, sir."

"He could have been motivated in that by a desire on his part to establish some kind of mental defense."

"He could have, sir."

Brackett pointed out that most of the tests Evans ran showed Robertson within normal ranges. But Evans noted Robertson had trouble with a test that showed impulsive responses and there were exceptions to the tests that showed normal behavior.

"The exceptions fit a pattern of frontal-lobe dysfunction," he said.

As the day wore on and the defense continued with its fourth psychiatric witness, some in the audience were growing weary. Wechsler tests, EEGs, brain mapping and the like seemed a bit dry. A local newspaper reported a woman in the audience leaned over to a friend and whispered, "This is getting as boring as the O.J. Simpson trial."

The subject of pharmacology came next through the testimony of Dr. Alexander Morton, an assistant professor in both the pharmacy and psychiatric departments at the Medical University of South Carolina. His specialty was psychopharmacology and substance abuse.

He said nothing gets the brain's attention any faster than smoking cocaine. People feel good when they first start using—high energy, positive—but then the impairment comes. People can become paranoid, angry and aggressive.

"They warn people in an emergency room to be careful because they can get beat up real easy," he said. Patients on drugs become violent, even those who were ordinarily meek.

Morton testified that Robertson told him he was drinking twelve to fourteen beers most evenings but had never experienced a seizure or withdrawal.

"Was he irritable in the morning when he was getting up?"

"I think he was not feeling particularly peppy. I don't know if he ever tried to cut down himself. I think he was at the point where he was still enjoying the drug," Morton said.

He was almost always drinking when he wasn't working and he continued to use drugs even though he was out of control.

"Some people if they get a DUI, they might say, 'Hey I've got a problem.' Some people if they go into jail, they might say, 'Hey, I really do have a problem' and then some people don't," Morton said.

He said James Robertson gave up important activities such as spending time with his family. He didn't play basketball or go to school.

"It is a medical disease. It does have a biological basis. One has to suspend logic to believe that, and everyone in here hopefully is working on a basis of logic, but when you try to make sense out of why people do the things that they do, it doesn't make sense. And people say, 'Well, they just need to stop, or they need to go to church more or they need to work harder, and that's not what we're talking about. Biology out of control and really the only way to treat it is to stop using, and stopping using is a massive task."

He said treatment could come in many ways, but his preference was an inpatient rehabilitation unit. Such places usually are able to keep the drugs away from the patient.

Other treatments include twelve-step groups such as Alcoholics Anonymous or something similar, counseling, stress management, avoiding situations and problem solving.

"If you've been drinking and drugging through this time that you learn how the world works—for me, it would be from twelve to twenty [when] you learn how the world works. You learn how to deal with your parents. You learn how to deal with peers. Figure out if they didn't work how to solve it. If you're drinking and drugging, you never learned it, so here you are a fifty-year-old man dealing with a problem of a fourteen-year-old."

Morton told the jury he reviewed the prescription records from CVS Pharmacy that were filled by members of the Robertson family. Terry Robertson's medications filled three sheets; Earl, Chip and James filled one each.

James Robertson had taken Lithium, Depakote and antibiotics. Earl was prescribed two antidepressants, antibiotics and skin products. He was on Serzone when he died, and he felt it had been helping.

Terry took medications for obsessive-compulsive disorder. She also took antidepressants, sleeping pills and antipsychotic drugs. On her list were Prozac, Lithium, Depakote, medications for high blood pressure, cholesterol, weight reduction medications and estrogen replacement.

Chip had been prescribed Ritalin, Serzone, Wellbutrin and Tegretol.

The family also had medications filled through Express, a mail order pharmacy company. They bought drugs in larger quantity by mail, including Xanax, antihistamines, and Cardiozyme for the heart.

Based on the medications and the records of doctors, Morton said he prepared a chart showing the psychological problems of the various family members.

Earl had depression, ADHD, anxiety. Terry had obsessive-compulsive disorder and bipolar disorder. James Robertson had some of the same genetics, ADD, bipolar, a little bit of obsessive-compulsive disorder. A full case would involve thoughts and compulsions that take over more than an hour a day. He didn't have that. He did abuse alcohol, Ritalin and marijuana. Chip had depression, ADD, alcohol abuse.

Under cross-examination from Pope, Morton said he talked to Robertson on March 11.

"Your description to the jury today of the defendant's psychosis that night being based at least in large part [on] him relating to you what happened."

"It is based on my clinical experience of working with approximately four thousand drug addicts that have cocaine as a major drug, and to know cocaine inside and out, and to see the consequences of cocaine intoxication and then seeing the few people—I only have two people in the clinic that are big people— who are taking Methylphenidate for attention deficit disorder. My population of folks are not using Ritalin as some of the younger adolescents."

"I understand that, sir," Pope said. "Again, to bring you back to my question, largely it came from this defendant as far as the acts he committed that night and the statement he gave these other doctors as to what happened that night."

"It came primarily from his report and past clinical experience where if you use this drug in large amounts, this will happen."

"You said based on your experience of what happens when people take large doses of the drug. Then again, I'm not trying to put words in your mouth, but that's how you know he was psychotic the night he killed his parents because he told you he took large amounts of the drug. Is that correct?"

"I'm relying totally on his self-report and the fact there were large amounts of drugs coming into the house. It looked like a drugstore actually. I don't mean to be facetious, but I've never seen that many prescriptions in those quantities being dispensed to a household."

Pope asked whether the prescriptions were for a four-year period. Morton said some were, but some were for a year. Under questioning, Morton also acknowledged that some of the drugs were for routine illnesses, upset stomach and the like, and that there were mistakes in some entries on the list.

"You can't say whether they took them?" Pope asked.

"That's true."

Pope looked at Morton's report as he spoke about Robertson's abuse of drugs, alcohol and even caffeine. He used his folksy, easygoing, self-effacing demeanor as he probed Morton's testimony.

"People do uncontrollable things that's unbelievable," Morton said, leaning back comfortably in the chair, his chin resting on his hand.

"Of course, you've said you've seen the pictures, and part of your diagnosis is based on [that] there must be something wrong with him, he must have something, he's done something this bad, is that correct?" Pope asked.

"I saw the pictures, and they were horrible."

"And that's what you indicated, you show it, and there must be some drug explanation, some explanation."

"There doesn't have to be, but here's someone that has bipolar disorder and addictive disorders, both of which can be treated, and I would just like the chance to educate people that if we would take his life I want to make sure that there's no question that he doesn't have a disorder that we could treat. If he doesn't have a disorder, then you make your own decision, but I think he has a biological disorder, two of which have caused him incredibly bad behavior, and I think it needs to be looked at. If it wasn't looked at here, it would have to be looked at again, I'm afraid."

"Basically, you're saying that he didn't receive sufficient treatment, in your judgment, to this point, is that correct?"

"He did not receive sufficient treatment," Morton said. "There have been other patients who did not receive adequate treatment from that physician. I looked at a document from Freedom of Information Act and Dr. McMeekin indeed was publicly reprimanded for his breach of ethics with two patients and his license was put under review for two years from '96 to '98 because of the way he prescribes medications and the way he indeed does not document what's going on, so I don't think he received good treatment, no."

"OK, not in that regard. And now that you've handed your indictment on Dr. McMeekin, tell me about Dr. Prier at the state hospital."

"I don't know Dr. Prier. I did not study . . . only studied the discharge summary."

"Are you aware he made a deal with Dr. Prier basically to play the game so he could get out? Are you aware of that?"

"No, I'm not. I am aware that patients when they are involuntarily committed, they quickly learn you can stay there or you can say the right things to get out."

When Dr. Alexander Morton stepped down, he had been on the stand for three hours and it was after seven o'clock in the evening.

Chapter 22

It was cloudy on Thursday, but by the time court reconvened, it was nearly 60 degrees.

It was perfect golfing weather. Not too hot. Not too sunny. But Dr. George Hook, a Rock Hill dentist who was a golfing buddy of Earl's, wasn't going to play golf. He was sitting in courtroom 1, asking for mercy for his pal's son. Hook told the jury he and Earl played golf together at least once or twice a month. He and Earl went on several golfing outings together each year.

"I think I might have been with Earl the last time that he played," Hook said. "We had a . . . We went out on a Sunday afternoon and he probably played the best that I think I can ever remember. He eagled the ninth hole. I missed a little short putt on the last hole and he won all the bets and this led to a funny thing later. Jimmy came to the office about three weeks before this tragedy. He had some terrible dental problems that had accumulated over time. Earl wanted to take care of these. Wanted to not have Jimmy go on with any problems. At the end of the golf match, Earl looked at me and smiled and said, 'Sure is nice to take my dentist's money.' After I saw Jimmy at the office and related to Earl on the phone, he said, 'Let's do it. I want to take care of it. I knew I wouldn't keep that money in my pocket very long.' This showed me that to the end what was important was making sure things were taken care of."

"What are you asking this jury for in regard to Jimmy Robertson with your knowledge of the family?"

Hook looked at the jury.

"I'm asking this jury for mercy," Hook said, raising his eyes to look at the ceiling. "May I expound?"

James Robertson cried. He bit his lips. He held his hand to his mouth. His temples bulged and he looked at one point like he was going to throw up.

"Yes."

"I knew Earl. He was a very good friend. I know that he cared. I'm asking you—not as the jury—because you represent all of us. Now you make the final decision, but you're representing all of us. Let's not be the last to throw the stones. Please show mercy."

Pope rose to cross-examine.

"Dr. Hook, have you been in the courtroom this week to hear what transpired, what took place in this case?"

"No, I have not been in the courtroom."

Linda Hook, George Hook's wife, also asked the court to show mercy, as did Julian McLaughlin Jr., who went to Oakland Avenue Presbyterian Church with the Robertsons and knew James Robertson from Boy Scouts.

"I did a lot of thinking about it and had to put some of my personal thoughts aside and thinking what Terry . . ."

"I have the same objection," Pope said, referring to the judge's ruling that witnesses could not speculate about what Terry or Earl Robertson would want to happen to their son. "Don't go over that," Hayes told Hancock.

McLaughlin acknowledged that he had had limited knowledge of Robertson once he became an adult and did not know the intricate details of the case.

The defense then called one of Robertson's junior-high teachers, who said Robertson's mother would never let him suffer the consequences of his actions.

"Mrs. Robertson would come to me personally and accost me as to why I did what I did in terms of discipline," said Michael Faulkner, a teacher at Catawba Christian School.

He taught Robertson in the seventh and eighth grades, and at that age, James obsessed on making everything perfect and he could not control his anger, the teacher testified. He told the mother, who in turn said, "There's nothing wrong with my children."

The defense shifted back to making the case for saving Robertson's life because he had a mental disorder and a family life no child should be forced to endure.

Toni Cascio, an assistant professor of social work at the University of South Carolina, sat in the witness-box, poised, with notes in hand. It was her first time testifying as an expert witness, yet she seemed calm and efficient. Cascio looked distinguished in a beige suit and silk blouse. Her near-black hair was cut short, her face framed in bangs.

Boyd asked her about her evaluation of James Robertson. She met with him three times, she said, once the previous November and twice in December. She said she also based her conclusions on interviews with other people who knew the Robertsons, including Earl's mother, Christine Robertson, family friends, teachers and school administrators and the assorted counselors who had examined Robertson and treated his parents.

Terry Robertson was bipolar and suffered from obsessive-compulsive disorder, Cascio testified. Terry Robertson had never openly admitted it, but her hallucinations, self-mutilation and suicidal thoughts led Cascio to believe that Terry had been sexually abused.

"She saw ice cubes turn into babies, red pills turn into worms, and another time, she saw a kid with a tail," Cascio testified.

Cascio did not say who she thought abused Terry Robertson. Terry's friends were horrified at the suggestion. They did not believe it for an instant and were angry that the defense would announce something so vile in such a public way. They felt angry with James Robertson for allowing it.

Cascio described Earl Robertson as a distant man with a bad temper. Terry was perceived by her children as the rich princess, while Earl was the guy from the other side of the tracks. Robertson was emotionally attached to his parents even as he acted like he hated them.

She testified that Robertson had been physically and emotionally abused by his parents, that he had witnessed domestic violence and suffered from impaired parental bonding.

"Jimmy came from a very chaotic home," Cascio said. "There was a variety of things going on, including physical abuse, mental abuse, as well as mental illness throughout."

Once his father became so angry with him, he held him over a balcony. Another time, the father, enraged with Chip, tore his shirt. James Robertson's problems, she said, caused him to seek refuge in drugs and alcohol. He gambled and displayed antisocial behavior.

She speculated that James Robertson had been sexually, physically and psychologically abused. He can feel his own pain, Cascio testified, but not that of others. His home life was so bad, he saw no way out but violence.

"Jimmy's adolescence was very difficult. Kids would shun him, and he had a difficult time forming relationships."

He fell asleep, beginning as a toddler and continuing for many years after that, by banging his head on a headboard. Europe, Robertson told her, was the best twelve months of his life because he had friends. Boyd asked her if Robertson's problems explained what happened.

"It doesn't give a direct explanation, but when people have problems, they turn to drugs."

She said he saw his parents fighting and his mother withdraw from the world. After Terry's mother died, Terry started having more troubles. She didn't cook. The children cleaned the house. She gained eighty pounds in a year

James Robertson didn't have many friends. "He was an outcast," Cascio said. "All of these factors led him to start relying on drugs, which in turn led him to what happened later on."

Boyd told the judge he had no further questions and walked back to the defense table to sit between Robertson and Hancock.

Pope rose. He organized his black notebooks and papers, lining up some on the edge of the wall beside the prosecution table. He carried a notebook with him as he walked toward Cascio. He laid the notebook on a stand. When he asked about her report, she explained again that her report was based on interviews and reports from medical personnel. She also had the Robertsons' insurance claims.

"Terry was sexually abused?" Pope asked.

"Most likely, yes. She shows a number of indicators," Cascio responded evenly.

"You're not saying she was. You're saying 'most likely.'"

"There is nothing definite that she was, but yes, there are many indications that she was."

"You said 'probably' and 'maybe' and it can be an 'indication,' but you can't say she was sexually abused. You have no direct evidence," Pope said again, reinforcing his view that Cascio was speculating.

Finally she said, "Yes."

Pope worked to undermine the veracity of Cascio's work by making light of anything said by Earl Robertson's mother, an aged grandmother. He wondered whether she had talked to Earl's supervisor. She had not. And he raised the issue that many of the psychological evaluations done on Terry were done in the period between 1995 and 1997, the time when James Robertson was out of control.

Under Pope's cross-examination, she acknowledged that the incident in which Earl held his son over a balcony involved Earl bending him backward, not forward over the rail.

"You'd agree there's a difference?" Pope asked.

"Yes," she responded.

"You didn't see major physical abuse," Pope said.

"Not the worst I've ever seen. However, when you combine physical and emotional abuse, you get more negative outcomes."

She said Earl Robertson often yelled at his sons and told them they were dumb.

Cascio testified that Terry Robertson did not hold her son accountable for his misbehavior from the time he was a small child and was inconsistent in her discipline.

Pope, looking at Cascio's report, asked about the many times she couched her statements.

"'Often,' 'probably,' 'maybe,' 'sometimes.' When we get to something that's concrete, [you] tell me that. Do you understand what I'm asking?" Pope said.

"It doesn't work that way," Cascio responded.

Pope pointed out that her report mentioned confrontations between the parents, yet she only specifically discussed one.

"Does it say the children were present?" Pope asked.

"No," Cascio said.

"Does it say when it happened?" Pope asked.

"I don't recall the exact date in Skip Meyer's notes, but it was in the notes, so it does have a date," she responded.

"In fairness to this jury, and I'm not trying to niggle you on this, there is not more than one," Pope said.

"Yes," she said.

"You have that one incident," Pope said, trying to reinforce his point that Cascio had nothing concrete.

Reading from her notes, Pope said, "'Jimmy Robertson was beaten by both parents. Terry was known to hit Jimmy and pull his hair. It began in early childhood.'"

Looking up from the notebook, Pope asked, "Didn't Jimmy deny physical abuse?"

"Yes, but that's not uncommon," Cascio responded. "That's part of the pattern. That's how kids react."

She explained that children in such situations often don't see the parents' actions as abuse. Robertson was beaten with a belt several times a week from the time he was small and had unexplained marks on his back. When he banged his head on the headboard as he drifted off to sleep, "Earl would snatch him out of bed," she said, adding that Robertson had three unexplained head injuries.

But Pope suggested that there was no way to know who hit Robertson or how the injuries were inflicted.

Robertson was angry with his mother because she did not protect him from his father, Cascio said. One time, she told him she wished he had never been born.

"But then she apologized," Pope said.

"Yes, but the damage had been done. It wasn't an isolated incident," Cascio said.

"What other incidents do you have?"

"There were other emotional abuses going on in the family."

"Reported by Jimmy and Chip?"

"Yes."

He also never felt his father loved him, Cascio said.

She explained that she believed there was sexual abuse going on because the boys took showers with their parents when they were eleven and twelve years old.

"That is developmentally inappropriate," she said.

Pope stepped up the pressure on Cascio.

"As far as domestic abuse, there's not much to support that, is that correct?"

"The indicators all total, the whole is greater than the sum of its parts. Jimmy shows characteristics of people who have been through these things."

Pope said, "It's a kind of synergistic thing, each part grabs onto the next, but as you break down the parts, it doesn't stand alone; it doesn't even stand up, is that correct? Domestic violence—we've got one incident out of a whole lifetime, is that correct?"

"That we know of."

"OK, otherwise we're speculating. We're going backward. We're here today, so there must be something wrong. Is there an evaluation for just plain mean—just plain greedy?"

"I don't understand what you mean by that," she said.

She talked about the marks on his back and the head banging.

"Although they appeared to be well functional to the outside world, there were serious problems inside that household," she said.

James Robertson did not form friendships easily, she said.

"This lack of attachment is almost an ironic disorder," she said. "You can feel your pain but not the pain of others."

James Robertson sought solace in substance abuse and saw violence as his only alternative.

Pope turned to Cascio's notes. She had taken them during her interviews with Robertson, and Pope had asked the judge for permission to see them. Hayes agreed. The night before, when the notes were delivered, Brackett and Pope eagerly read through them. They could not believe what they were reading. Robertson's own words. They highlighted and highlighted, and highlighted some more, all the information they believed would help their case. Then they started whittling it down. There was so much, Brackett remembered later.

Many years later, when Pope reflected on his cross-examination of Cascio, which his office uses as a training film, Pope described his feelings as being like a wide receiver standing alone in the end zone as the pass sails near. The only thought is just don't drop the ball.

In the notes, Robertson described himself as a "pretty smart guy" who hated college. His parents forced it down his throat. He flunked out of college on purpose to get back at his parents. Robertson knew that his failure was of particular pain to his father. He called them clueless about drugs and complained they overreacted to his drug use. They routinely bailed him out of his troubles. His father, in particular, would not let him fail financially; therefore he had no understanding of or respect for money. He ran tabs at bars he couldn't pay, didn't pay bills and stole money from his father's wallet. He had had ten jobs.

Cascio said James Robertson was emotionally immature, too much to leave his parents and Rock Hill, which he said would have been better for him. "'Ever since I was real young, everything was a big deal,'" she quoted Robertson as saying. "'If I didn't make my bed, the roof came off.'"

"There was nothing preventing him from getting out from under Mama and Daddy's table, was there not?" Pope asked.

"No."

Pope asked her to turn to the pages where Robertson recounted the night before and morning of the murder. Robertson told her he was taking Ritalin and called his brother at 2:30 in the morning. He wanted Chip to come home for Thanksgiving. He called Moon and asked her for $75 to bring Chip home. She offered instead to drive there and get Chip.

"'Meredith was infatuated with Jimmy. Would have done anything for him,'" Cascio read from her notes.

"'Somehow it led to "I'm going to do it," but he needed assistance,'" Cascio said. "'Discussion of whether she's going to help him. Discussed which bat to use, not wooden, signed and autographed, didn't want to ruin it.'"

"Did you say 'bat'?"

"Yes."

"I'm sorry, ma'am, I didn't understand," Pope said, wanting her to repeat what she had just said about choosing a bat based on its value. He wanted to be sure the jury heard the callousness of the remark. She repeated it, then said, "'He condensed two bottles of Tilex, sat in the room and waited for father to shower.'"

"His intentions were to do what?" Pope asked.

"'Kill Mom while Dad was in the shower.'"

"Why was that?"

"There would be noise."

"What did he do next?"

"'Took phone off hook, laid one knife in hallway.'"

"Why was that?"

"'In case Dad came in.'"

"OK, where did he go next?"

"Went to bedroom."

"And did what?"

"'Struggled with Mom for a while.'"

"What did she start doing?"

"Screaming."

"Who was she screaming for?"

"Earl."

"'It was getting at me to hear her scream,'" Pope read from the notes.

"Yes."

"Now it bothers him that that was the last thing they saw before they died," Cascio said referring to James Robertson.

"Yes."

"He was in a rage like a madman."

"He came downstairs," Cascio said.

"Then what did he say?"

"'One down, one to go.'"

"What did he do with the bat?"

"Put it at the top of the stairs."

"When he put the bat at the top of the stairs, what did he do?"

"Sat and waited."

"Sat and waited what?"

"'Sat and waiting with the hammer, like I was standing on the other side of myself watching me.'"

"Tell them what he did next."

"Sprayed Tilex in father's eyes and hit him with the hammer."

"Ma'am, is that what it says?"

"'Sprayed Tilex in eyes and buried claw hammer in head.'"

"What did father do?"

"'Father put up a fight with hammer stuck in his head.'"

"What happened next?"

"'Eventually Dad fell to ground. Hit two hundred times with hammer and bat.'"

"What's his next statement?"

"'Twenty-two years of rage came out.'"

"He said it was overkill and he kept on and on and on and on," Pope said.

"Yes."

"Then he went in the bedroom to check on her."

"Yes."

"What did he do to her?"

"He hit her with a hammer to make sure she was dead."

"And Meredith thought he was going to kill her."

"Yes."

"OK, and heard a noise upstairs. What is that?"

"I don't know what was going on, but he heard noises upstairs."

James Robertson rubbed his eyes, dropped his head and put his hand on his forehead as Cascio replayed his words.

"What does he say?"

"It was his father breathing into the carpet, that's what he thought the noise was."

"OK, and what does he say next?"

"'How is he still living?'"

"OK, tell this jury what he did then."

"'Went to find a drill to end this madness.'"

"Did you say 'drill'?" Pope said, lingering on the word "drill" just enough to get the jury's attention. Several of them were so enthralled in the back-and-forth, the rhythm of the exchange, they moved their heads from one to the other as if they were at a tennis match.

"That's what it says, yes."

"You took this from talking to him?"

"Yes."

"What did he do next?"

"'Took bat upstairs and beat him again.'"

"And after that?"

"'Kicked with toe to see if he was dead.'"

"OK, and so that was the incident of the violence that he saw no other alternative other than this," Pope said, making the point that James Robertson had other options.

"That he might have, yes."

Pope had managed to get Cascio into a rhythm of words that made it sound as if Jimmy Robertson was testifying—incriminating—himself. Boyd and Hancock sat by helplessly. They had intended Cascio to help the defense by pulling some evidence threads together. She could tie the family dynamics with the drug use to explain in some way why Robertson had acted so heinously. Now she looked like the prosecution's star witness. Looking back, Boyd said Cascio's testimony was the most damaging in the trial.

"That went bad," Boyd said to Hancock.

Julius "Skip" Meyer, who earned his Ph.D. from the University of Florida, had been the family therapist for two years. He ran Carolina Counseling in Rock Hill, where Debbie Brisson worked and where Terry Robertson had become a regular.

James Robertson, in a gray suit, sat back casually in his seat, occasionally turning around to look at the audience behind him.

It was clear from the way Meyer sat and answered questions he was doing so under duress. He did not want to be there. He did not want to reveal the confidential conversations with three members of the Robertson family. In a monotone, he read, reading glasses low on his nose, directly from his office notes. He rarely looked up, even between questions. If he did, he looked at the court reporter, not at the lawyers or the jury as other witnesses did.

"'Jimmy was seen individually and collaterally with his parents—real concern for Jim is that he's been working an incredible amount of hours,'" he read. "'Reports to having worked thirty-three straight hours in his job, and of course I find this remarkable if not impossible. I stressed how Jim starts behaving and doing this; that it's ill advised because he lacks judgment and it will interfere with perception that he can do anything and do it all. That kind of mentality has gotten him into serious trouble in the past—kind of correlates that with having an extreme positive self-concept that sometimes interferes with his judgment and he does not think for himself clearly. The relationship between him and his father seemed to have dramatically improved. They are talking more and mom is becoming less involved in the relationship. No gambling. No indications of behavior related to gambling and overall feel that things are going well.'"

"All right," Hancock said. "On 3/23/95, sir."

"'Jim was seen in conjunction with his parents, one-hour collateral therapy session, overall trying to identify a scenario for Jim's depression, his irresponsible behavior, his inability to manage money and gambling difficulties. Overall it appears that his father is extremely frustrated with his son's behavior and the mother is very timid of how to deal with him. Ended the session by having the son give his ATM cards to his father. He does not have access to these cards, agreed to let him maintain control of his checking account with the implicit and explicit agreement with both parents that if he writes bad checks, forges any names, that he would have to suffer the consequences without his parents' help. Jim acknowledges that he believes his parents are serious at this point in time— indicated that in the past his parents would have made such a statement he would not have to put much faith in it. Also put the father in charge of his paycheck. This seemed to be agreeable with all parties although Jim was somewhat resistant to this idea. I will see them back hopefully within a week. I think this is critical time in treatment.'"

Hancock asked him to turn to Earl Robertson's records. Earl went to Meyer at Terry's urging. He felt frustrated. He felt he worked hard, saved his money and yet had a poor relationship with Terry, who wouldn't cook or even keep the house clean. His sons were a disappointment. They didn't respect him. His only joy was found on the golf course.

In most of the thirty-seven sessions, the doctor described Earl as "overwhelmed, stressed, depressed." He felt unappreciated, misunderstood and embarrassed by his family. He wanted stability, order, and found only chaos. His life was nothing like he dreamed it would be. He especially hated having to explain to people that his son was in jail. He wanted to go to sleep and not wake up.

"Let's start with, and this would probably be toward the back, 7/24/96," Hancock said.

"'Stressed, angry, feeling fed up with children's irresponsible behavior. Attests to being out of control as to how to deal with and manage his children. Spouse differs on his views.'

"'8/9/96: Stressed, family's falling apart, costing a lot of money, taking an emotional toll on wife and self. Encouraged Earl to do what is in Jimmy's best interest. Feels overwhelmed with shame and embarrassment and humiliation—feels that he has worked his whole life to be an upstanding citizen and now he feels he needs to move due to the embarrassment he feels. Conflict over how to deal with the children.'"

"It says 'children' there, doesn't it?" Hancock asked.

"Yes, sir."

"Both of them?"

"This is correct. I believe this is the time they were in trouble for breaking into the next-door neighbor's house."

"They both were in trouble for that," Hancock said.

"I believe so."

"And Jimmy was the one who went to jail for it."

"That's my understanding."

"As far as you know, Chip never was charged or even held responsible in any way."

"That's my understanding."

"'3/11/97: Stressed, anger, feels like life has been ruined by son. Not an hour goes by without feeling sad or angered at his son. Unable to differentiate Jimmy from self. Feels guilty, shame and humiliation.'"

"4/30/97, please, sir."

"'Animated, feels overwhelmed with son coming home, feels easily hurt, angers over Jimmy easily, feels total embarrassment, how to be protective/proactive with the family.

"'11/7/97: Presents with anger, hopelessness—fears the worst for Chip—just wants to be done with his children—thinks Jimmy might be deteriorating—questions how well spouse is doing—fears she will overcommit self with the holidays—dates of her mother's birthday and the holidays without her parents will create stress, yet all the pressure is on him to deliver and they want to make him the fall guy, what do they expect. Hope to get a refund from Chip's school. Good sign, he was going out to the school band presentation last night. Thinking about tonight going to the Rock Hill–Northwestern game. Work stress is tolerable, however expresses humiliation over Chip's phone calls, supports limits he is contemplating setting.'"

"Let's go to Terry's record, sir. Let's go to 8/8/95." On that date, Terry Robertson had been seeing Meyer for about a month. Her first visit, on July 12, 1995, came at the referral of Dr. Hayne McMeekin, a psychiatrist. She had never been in therapy before, although she had taken part in self-help groups offered by her church.

Jimmy Robertson had been seeing Meyer in weekly sessions for about four months. On Terry's first visit, she told Meyer she was depressed and worried excessively. It stemmed from Jimmy flunking out of Georgia Tech. Her son's failure caused her husband to be angry and frustrated, and Terry's natural tendency was to protect her son.

"She keeps the peace," Meyer wrote in his notes, which were admitted into evidence at the trial. "She is overwhelmed, withdrawing."

Terry Robertson had difficulty sleeping and felt her life changed when her father died seven years earlier. Terry also told Meyer she did not trust her husband. The record does not say why.

Friends of Terry's had no idea of what was to come or how bad it would look for their friend by the time court ended that day.

Meyer flipped through the scores of pages until he found the notes from that August day.

"'Depressed in Grand Rapids over feeling she has bad children. Depressed on and off—currently no interest in outside activities, friends, recent loss of appetite and medical problems, fears future of her health, probably will be having surgery. Check on marital problems when Jimmy was one year old.'"

Hancock said, "8/9/95. Do you know when they were in Grand Rapids, Michigan?"

"No, I do not. I don't know the time period. It was after they were in California."

"But she indicated she was depressed in Grand Rapids over feelings she had bad children?" Hancock asked, his voice rising at the end, incredulously.

"That's what my notes indicate."

"Do you know how old her children were then?"

"No, I would give a guesstimate of somewhere between six to eight."

"She was indicating she had bad children back then."

"That's what this would reflect."

"There was a reference to when Jimmy was one year, would you clarify that?"

"That was a note to myself probably at that time. Being a family therapist, I look for major life-cycle events that occur that change family dynamics.

Usually the birth of a child is one of those life-changing events."

James Robertson stared down at the floor and chewed on his finger. He looked around at the people in the audience and into the camera of Court TV.

Hancock asked him to read the entry for August 9, that same year.

"'Continue to track the history of movement of the family. California was a positive experience and it helps getting away from family. It sounds as when Jimmy was born, she felt a great deal of pressure of how to "properly" raise Jimmy from her mother—this appeared to cause some type of fear—fear of doing the wrong thing with holding him. It sounds as if there were the normal type of marital adjustments for a new baby to be made—except more outside influences.'"

The notes say Terry turned to her family, not Earl, for support. She also told Meyer her sex life with Earl changed after the baby was born, a situation she had a hard time adjusting to. Meyer notes that Terry cried on and off through the session. Over the two years Terry Robertson saw Meyer, sometimes she would see him every other day, other times once a week or twice a month. In all, she had 188 sessions with Meyer.

Her husband saw Meyer just about every week, from July 3, 1996, until November 21, 1997, four days before he died.

In the early days of Terry Robertson's therapy, she told Meyer she felt nearly immobilized by depression. She blamed herself for all the problems in her household. On her third visit, Meyer asked her to make a list of fifteen things she did right as a parent. The record does not show that she made the list.

Instead, she came back two days later "stressed, depressed." She felt like running away. In August 1995, Terry told her therapist she wanted to die. She found solace in listening to the radio station WWMG, Magic 96.1, an oldies station from Charlotte, North Carolina. In September, Terry Robertson told Meyer she had thoughts of suicide, thoughts she repeated through the month and into October. Early that month, she agreed to begin taking medication.

During a two-hour session on October 5, 1995, Meyer wrote that Terry felt like she was manic-depressive. She worked fiendishly as president of the PTA for her children's school and had "grandiose" ideas. She spent too much money and regularly bounced checks. She bought items and then left them in the bag.

Later that month, Terry told Meyer she wondered why she was so attracted to Earl in college. She quickly added her parents thought he was the "right material." She also told Meyer she bought razor blades and cut herself on the leg. She was seeing Meyer every other day.

In November, Terry Robertson told Meyer her goals for therapy were to understand what happened to her, how she could help her boys, whether she should separate from her husband and how to handle bipolar illness.

By the end of the month, Terry was making more serious comments about suicide. On December 5, she was hospitalized. Earl visited her, but her sons did not. She was discharged four days before Christmas.

Some of her closest friends did not know she had been in therapy and they did not know the depths of her despair. She felt she had failed as a mother, daughter and wife. She felt she was a loser her whole life and that if her friends truly knew who she was, they would not like her. Her mother was a perfectionist, who ruined her life, she told the counselor, but then felt guilty about saying bad things about her mother.

Terry no longer found joy in anything in her home. She did not want to clean or cook or have sex with her husband. Terry was distressed about her husband's comments about her weight.

"I want the floor to open up and swallow me," she told the doctor. Her stomach stayed upset and her hair was falling out. She had headaches and sometimes hallucinated, hearing her mother's voice. In a trash bag, she collected items that she could kill herself with: a hairdryer, razor, aspirin, pillowcase. She visualized ways of killing herself, looking at trees in the yard to see which were tall enough to hang from. Hopelessness filled her soul.

In an undated letter she wrote to Meyer about a year into her therapy, Terry confided that she considered herself promiscuous. She said she played around with sex through all her "growing up years"—sometimes having several sexual relations going on at the same time. She did not have actual intercourse until she married Earl.

She said their honeymoon was fun, but there were "some problems." They rocked along in their marriage, she said, but "then came Lynn and Don." The letter does not say precisely what she meant, but the implication is one or both had affairs. They both tried hard to rebuild their marriage after that.

Recently, she said, she had had no interest in sex

with her husband. She was either too angry or aggravated with him or too tired or depressed.

Hancock asked Meyer to read from the session on January 14, 1997, ten months before the murder.

"'1/14/97: I have a lot of anger towards Earl. I am furious at Earl for what I think he has done to the kids. Chip never felt comfortable with Dad. . . .'"

"She was furious at Earl 'when I think what he has done to the kids'?" Hancock asked.

"That is correct."

"Any elaboration on that, sir?"

"My memory was they went to some sort of vacation to the mountains and Earl had grabbed Chip by the shirt and kind of put him up against the wall and said something to the effect of, 'You think you're man enough or something to take me on or pay attention to me one way or another.'"

"It makes other reference to physical confrontation, is that correct, sir?"

"Yes, sir."

Hancock asked about the February 6, 1997, session.

"'From age eight, remembers engaging in self-punishing behavior—in apparent reaction to parental conflict, generalize her behavior to Jimmy, camp incident when fifteen about mail—got a far-off look when talking about guilt, embarrassment,'" Meyer read.

And on August 26, 1997, Meyer suggested that Earl lie across the bed and read while Terry read.

"'It's really great having Jimmy home,'" Meyer's notes say. "'He is helpful. Not presenting particularly overwhelmed. However, she got flushed several times during session, also she would start shaking—especially in response to discussing spouse's anger. Continue to set goals. To strive for meeting their children's needs. Wants to be blind to their behavior but has made excellent progress.'"

On cross-examination, Brackett asked Meyer whether he considered the incident in the mountains physical abuse.

Meyer said he did not. He also said he believed Terry was concerned about her children in Michigan because they were acting out, but he did not have any recollections of what they were doing.

Meyer sat impassively as Brackett shuffled through papers.

"During this time period from '95 to '97, how old were Chip and Jimmy?"

"Um, I'd have to look that up."

"Can you give me a guesstimate?"

"I think Chip must have been eighteen or nineteen in '95, getting ready to go to college and Jimmy was twenty-one."

"So, when Mr. Hancock was saying they were doing these things around the kids and this was happening to the kids, they weren't children back then, were they?"

"They were of age."

"And as a matter of fact, they were helping them even after they were old enough to get kicked out of the house by bringing them to your office and trying to get counseling for them and so forth, is that correct?"

"Correct."

"Now, you spoke to Ms. Cascio of the defense team."

"That's correct."

"How would you characterize her questioning regarding these notes and so forth?"

"She was pleasant and polite."

"Was she really interested in getting to the bottom of this or was she digging for dirt?" Brackett asked.

Hancock jumped in. "I object."

"No, I'll overrule it. It's cross-examination," Hayes said.

Meyer responded by looking at Brackett, his reading glasses still perched on his nose: "She appeared to be interested in whether or not I felt Terry was sexually abused, and looking at some passages of ours of aggressive, the screaming and yelling, the anger in the home."

"But it's fair to say she didn't have any real interest in getting a truth of what the home life was like."

"Your Honor, I'm going to object as to what she was trying to do," Hancock said, the pitch of his voice rising.

"I think he can answer that," Brackett said, "based on his conversations with her."

"Rephrase the question."

"Did it appear from her questioning of you that she was trying to get a total picture?"

"I think she was focusing on problem areas."

Meyer said he knew Terry Robertson was also seeing Dr. Hayne McMeekin and receiving "augmentation therapy," a combination of medications to help control her mental disorders. Meyer also said he believed the Robertsons had finally gotten a handle on their lives. They were working as a team to set limits for their sons. Terry had become more open and honest with her husband, not keeping information from him, as she had in the past, about sending money to Chip and the like.

According to the records Meyer submitted to the

court, Terry Robertson's last session was on October 6, 1997, more than a month before the murders. She told him there was a lot of arguing going on in her home, but she was staying focused. She had thrown out all her old prescription medicines and gone out to dinner with a friend. She seemed rested and relaxed.

But then she made a cryptic comment to Meyer. "If I were mom, I think I would want to make up for it. I would feel like I would be stabbing my mother with a knife. You don't know how stern my mother could be, remembers incredible stomach spasms."

A church member, Harold "Buzzy" Hall, who was in the Robertsons' Sunday school class and was Jimmy's basketball coach in high school, described Jimmy Robertson as different from other kids.

"He was kind of a loner, a little bit standoffish, a little bit off to the sides from the rest of the kids on the team."

"What are you asking of this jury?"

"I'm asking for *mercy,*" Hall said, emphasizing the word "mercy."

"I knew Jimmy as a smart young man, very intelligent, and I think Jimmy could be an asset to other folks that are in incarceration as far as an educational asset. Teaching people, helping others. I'm asking for mercy."

Paige McRight, an associate pastor at Oakland Avenue Presbyterian Church since July 1997, took the stand. She knew Terry Robertson from college but had only talked to Earl on the phone once. When Robertson was brought back to Rock Hill from Pennsylvania, McRight began visiting him in prison.

She estimated she saw him six times and she wrote to him.

"With all that you know, what are you asking this jury to do?"

"I'm asking this jury to spare Jimmy's life," she said, turning to face the jury, "to grant him mercy. Knowing what I know . . . knowing what I know about his parents and their hopes and dreams for their children and their dedication to them. Knowing what I know about his intelligence, I think their memories, their lives, their dreams, can be better honored by his being imprisoned and his making whatever he can of use to the world."

Chapter 23

As court was gaveled into session Friday morning, most everyone knew the end was near. Robertson came into court dressed in charcoal slacks, a navy blue blazer, blue shirt and patterned tie, the image of a college frat boy.

After a few perfunctory witnesses, Boyd told the judge the defense had finished its case.

"Before you do that, Mr. Robertson, I discussed with you on two occasions, really three counting the guilt phase, that you have a right to testify if you wish before this jury. You also have the right to remain silent. If you testify, you will be subject to cross-examination by the state and your prior offenses which have already been brought into the record they could ask you about those for the purpose of impeaching your credibility, not for anything regarding the sentence. Now they can use certain things regarding your past that are indicative of your character. But you have a right to testify or you have the absolute right to remain silent. If you chose your constitutional right to remain silent, I will tell the jury, as I did in guilt phase, they cannot consider that or factor that into their deliberation. You understand that."

"Yes."

"What is your decision?"

"I waive my right to testify at this time."

The prosecution called one rebuttal witness, Dr. Jeffrey McKee, a forensic psychologist, who told the jury about psychotic behavior. He said Robertson was not experiencing a psychotic episode or bipolar episode when he killed his parents.

"What specifically about the events of that night lead you to believe the defendant knew right from wrong?" Brackett asked.

"When a forensic psychologist does an assessment of the defendant's recognition or capacity to distinguish right from wrong, we look at the behavior that's reported of the defendant either by the defendant or witnesses before the particular incident, during the particular incident and after the particular incident. In my opinion, Mr. Robertson did know right from wrong."

Pope rose to wrap up his case.

"Ladies and gentlemen, I say that when you get down to your verdict, is it one of two things: either you buy that it's a combination of Ritalin psychosis and Terry and Earl being bad parents that either disciplined their kids too much or didn't discipline them enough, a bad family; him not having any breaks, him not having any opportunities, him getting the short end of the stick all of his life from the time that he can't remember—when he was banging his head—all the way through to the present, or he's a spoiled rich kid who could not wait to receive his inheritance.

"You heard the evidence; you heard the testimony. . . . You've got to separate the wheat from the chaff."

He scoffed at Dr. Pincus's psychological tests and

reminded the jury that Pincus was paid to be in the courtroom and paid to find a reason to explain what happened.

"Some things don't have explanations," Pope said. "We can try to fit it in. We can try to talk about motive. We can try to find motivation, but maybe sometimes people are just greedy and they're just evil."

Pope acknowledged that Robertson was manic-depressive, but he said many people have that disorder and get along fine in life every day. They don't murder their parents. He also said Robertson was not addicted to drugs and the evidence is that he threw fifteen Ritalin in the Dumpster in Maryland.

"There is such a thing as drug psychosis, but this is not one of them," Pope said. "This is what you call an excuse."

Pope said Robertson beat up his brother when he was not on drugs, proving Ritalin did not make him violent.

"It was clear that Terry basically went through hell the last three years of her life," Pope said. "And you remember the counselor said she was kind of coming out of it. They were starting to make some plans. They were starting to put some structure on those kids. They were starting to say they're not going to run their lives. They're going to take charge. They were going to set some parameters.

"They dragged Terry through the mud. Up and down and talk about all the medications, all the things that are happening piled together, all the medications that came into that house. But when you pull it apart, what is it you're seeing. Three years. She was going through a tough time, but in the meantime she was having to deal with [James]. She was having to deal with Chip."

Terry would have been horrified to know all her private thoughts had been aired, he said.

One incident of physical abuse, two incidents of fighting with the boys over twenty years of marriage.

"Terry was crucified. Earl was crucified. They're starting with the claw hammer and working backward."

The defense talked about Terry as being sexually abused, he said.

"Terry has been raped. She was raped in this courtroom," Pope said, shouting, "when they take her through this based on his actions. I've got an alternative for violence. Why doesn't Jim get off his rear end and get out and get a job?"

Pope lowered his voice.

"They did everything they could do for him, but he was like a leech—talk about physical abuse, talk about mental abuse. They still took care of him. And he continued to drain them. He drained them physically. He drained them emotionally, and he drained every drop of blood out of their body."

With his arms folded in front of his body as he stood in front of the jury, Pope said, "You know Jim had that fear of Daddy spending his inheritance. I think I've said this earlier, you know his dad came from mill hill. I hope that doesn't offend anybody. I grew up in Leslie, so I think I can say 'mill hill' if I want to. But you know Earl worked for everything he had, and this man—he was working, and he was saving, and he had two kids who were sharp as tacks and they could do anything they wanted."

And all Earl wanted was to retire and buy a golf course.

"Jim was spending that insurance money," Pope said. "Jim was spending that inheritance money before they had ever found the bodies."

Pope said the crime scene showed a method to Robertson's actions, which were not the actions of a "wild ape," as Robertson called himself.

Pope walked over to the table where the evidence had been stored and picked up the bat, sheathed in a heavy clear plastic bag.

"The first thing you have to do is you have to choose a weapon 'cause you're going to kill both your parents and you've got to decide if this is the best instrument of death."

He looked down at the bat in his hands.

"You know a pistol's pretty quick."

Snapping his fingers, he said, "Pop Mama in the head."

Snap.

"Pop Daddy in the head. Its over. It goes right back to him saying twenty years of hatred coming out. Twenty-two years of anger. This seems like a pretty good implement. You've got two bats to choose from, but we don't want to use the wooden autographed bat. Why wouldn't he use the wooden autographed bat? The autograph bat might be worth something."

Pope retraced the crime. He reminded the jury Robertson wore socks on his hands so he wouldn't leave fingerprints.

"Is that a smart man? Is that a thinking man?" He had done it before when he broke into his neighbor's house.

"He put those socks over his hands and he creeps up those stairs."

He displayed the note Robertson left on the kitchen table on the overhead projector for the jury to see.

"You know what they didn't find on that note? Anybody's blood. Anybody's blood. When Jim's down there picking out bats and picking up hammers and looking at different items, he thought he'd just jot a little note down on a pad to kind of lay out his alibi. So he gets the phone off the hook and he has his note laying up there and he puts a knife in the hall just in case Dad came and he works on Terry. This is the one he loved the most and he cuts her, he beats her, and then he goes downstairs again—one down, one to go. And he laid the bat at the top of the stairs.

"Earl's still in the shower. Terry screamed for help. Jim beat her and bludgeoned her and cut her to death. Goes back upstairs and he sits and waits. He's not enough of a man to take Earl straight on. Earl's in there, getting ready to head out to work."

He disabled his father with Tilex, Pope said.

"He buried the hammer into Earl's head. Did he go down? No, ma'am. No, sir. Keep fighting and he puts Earl down. Twenty years of rage. A man who always bailed him out. A mother who always took care of him.

"Do you remember why he took the bat to him again? He heard him breathing into the carpet from downstairs and he beats again, again, again. The man and the woman that brought him into this world. The man and woman who gave him everything. The man and woman who were so proud of this boy.

"And he goes into the bedroom to check on Mom

and he hits her with the hammer to make sure she's dead. Something he didn't tell us. Dr. Sexton told us. He goes back and cuts her again and again and again.

"Slashing cuts, not wild-ape cuts, slow and deliberate cuts, cuts across here," Pope said as he traced his index finger across the side of his face so forcefully it left a red mark.

"Again and again, the woman who brought him into this world. We won't have any physical evidence of this, but he tells Ms. Cascio that ultimately he thought about going to get a drill because Earl just wouldn't die. Finally Earl's dead, so he goes downstairs, this madman, this wild ape, he goes downstairs and he takes a shower and he washes the blood off of him and he bags up his evidence."

James Robertson sat back in his chair impassively.

Pope talked about Moon's credibility. He reminded the jury that Robertson had bragged to a social worker: "'Meredith was infatuated with me; she'd do anything I want.' Ladies and gentlemen, that one sentence has presented Meredith Moon's predicament better than I ever could. It's crazy. You say, 'Run, Meredith, get away, get out of the house, do something, tell the lady at the Peach Stand to help.' He had a hook. Good-looking, rich kid; poor, overweight Meredith. They made a big deal about how big she was. He had her hooked and he felt you couldn't convict on her testimony alone. Meredith Moon's going to pay dearly, pay for being totally fooled, pay for being a big girl in love. She made a mistake and she will pay."

Pope said he expected James Robertson to talk to the jury and asked them to put him under scrutiny, to ascertain what kind of a man he was. Hancock had compared the Robertsons to the Cleaver family, and Pope said the family probably was, but James Robertson was Eddie Haskell, not one of the sons. He was the one who presented a sweet face to some and a mischievous one to others. Pope reminded the jury that he tried to trick Erin Savage out of coming to court the other day. Use that to judge his credibility, Pope said.

"He can feel his pain," Pope said, his voice rising. "He's not happy because he's not living in a condo. He's not going to Europe. You may see some tears. I submit to you they are crocodile tears and I beg you, beg you, not to be swayed.

"The man that will stand before you is the same man that most graciously killed Mom because he couldn't live with her knowing that he killed Dad, leaving her all alone," Pope said, holding a picture of Terry's body for the jury to see. "Does that sicken you to the core? So, I beg you don't be swayed.

"Ladies and gentlemen, the truth of the matter is Jimmy started killing Terry and Earl long, long, long before November 1997. He failed out of college to prove a point. He used things to provoke Earl. 'Well, what if I rob a bank.' Every one of us has our weak spot. Every one of us has our tender spot. Here was their weak spot. They wanted a family. Where was their tender spot? They wanted a family that could achieve things they hadn't achieved, a family that could do things they haven't done. The same thing we all want our children to have—a better life, a better opportunity."

He talked about Terry and Earl's wills. They set up a trust for their sons.

"It's almost pitiful. It basically says something to the

effect should I predecease my husband it goes to him and so forth. Leave the estate and money to the benefit of my two children of whom I am most proud. It's really kind of pathetic, isn't it? We've been here a long time together. I was riding home last night thinking about it. . . . My dad's a big man. My dad used to tan my hide. Last night, I was riding, thinking this whole thing is so confusing. We don't want to think the neighborhood kid does this. We don't want to think that people like us can ever do these things. Puts you off kilter. Puts you in disarray. Lost my mother right after I got out of law school. My father had just turned eighty. I thought about things. He's still taking care of me. I'm married. I've got kids. He'll be calling to tell me how he bought some formula or he's thinking about this or wanting to do that. I'm thirty-six, thirty-seven, and long ago made my own way in life, and he loves me so much that he still takes care of me. I called him last night; I said, 'Daddy, I just want to thank you.' He said, 'Son, I do it because I love to.'"

Pope's face turned red and tears welled in his eyes.

"You have to believe that Terry and Earl loved these children more than they loved their life. You know, friends have come in. They're not jurors. They can't be fair and impartial, knowing Terry and Earl, and asking for mercy. Terry and Earl have given these boys and given and given and given their life's blood. Now they have the gall to come into this courtroom and ask Terry and Earl to give again. Won't be a mom in here begging for Jim's life. There won't be a dad in here begging for Jim's life. Jim's taken care of that.

"And I often say if you don't return a death verdict, then it's a mockery to the lives that were lost, but I'm not going to say that. The truth of the matter is the mockery began long, long ago when this man lied at every turn. The mockery carried on. . . . Terry was a private person; Earl was a proud man. The mockery carried on when they tore them wide open in this courtroom to somehow excuse what this man's done."

Pope pointed at Robertson, who looked as if he were going to cry.

"Ladies and gentlemen, when it's your responsibility—and I don't envy it—it's not about Terry and Earl anymore. It's about this community. You from all walks of life are the voice of this community and it's your determination, not on passion, not on prejudice, no friend to reward, no enemies to punish. You determine what price this crime has. You determine what the ultimate penalty should be. I submit to you, if this case does not beg for the death penalty, there is no case that begs for the death penalty.

"Ladies and gentlemen, Terry begged for her life. She pleaded for her life. Earl fought for his life and I can't help but think [when] the alarm went off at six this morning and I go get in the shower and I'm thinking about this trial and I can't hear a thing in the shower and I'm thinking about my close. What was Earl thinking about? Another day at work, wishing he could go play golf. Her flesh and blood, her son who she had given everything to.

"Ladies and gentlemen, that day Terry's screams went unheard, not by the Langleys across the street, not by the friends, who loved them so, not by her husband. She screamed for her protector, but he couldn't hear her screams. This case—this case screams out like Terry screamed. I beg you to hear it. It's not an easy decision. Please summon the strength to answer that scream with a verdict that speaks the truth. This man deserves death."

Thomas Pope had been speaking for an hour and twenty minutes.

Bill Hancock rose slowly from his seat and walked toward the jury.

"It is one of the most unusual cases that anyone probably in the United States has ever been involved in. You can look over there, you can tell the cameras, the reporters—everybody's here watching us and what we do. The solicitor has asked you due to the circumstances to authorize the state to kill Jimmy Robertson in the manner in which is chosen," Hancock said, walking over to stand in front of Robertson and pointing at him.

"He told you something else. He told you about his daddy. He told you if I heard it right, that's what parents do. They give life. I want to tell you something and it has been intimated that in a case of this nature that we should do less than our job and I want to remind you of something I told you about in opening arguments. I told you I didn't revel in this task, and I knew what was coming, and I told you it was no fun, and it had to be done because of the circumstances of this case because you have the decision to put him to death.

"I also told you talking to Mr. Skip Meyer one of the last questions I asked that doesn't make Earl a bad man, does it? That doesn't make Terry a bad woman. They weren't bad people. They contributed to their community. They did everything they should do. They could not control a lot the good Lord gave them, that's all there is to it. They couldn't control it. The solicitor talked about his father and what had been done, but maybe his father didn't have bipolar mental illness. Maybe his mother didn't have mutilation instincts. Those are things you've got to consider.

"But he talked about his daddy and being there. I'll talk about my mama. She's just as important to me, and no matter what I may have done if I was sitting where Jimmy is, my mama would say, 'Give Billy a chance.' That's what Billy's here to do and that's to give Jimmy a chance. You've got two choices. Two and only two. This is a horrible crime. I can't look at those pictures and sit there and not say this is a rascal. The same thing the solicitor said. The solicitor said it's confusing. It's pathetic. Good gracious, what was done to these people defies the imagination. That's why we're here. If you never ask why, you never arrive at what is a just conclusion.

"There may never be a rational or sane explanation of a crime of this nature, but we attempt and we try and we beg to understand it. The solicitor is begging you. I'm not begging you. I'm begging to be given or to find the ability to understand everything in the human mind. We can't do it. And that's what this case is about. That's what it is about, and to do it, you've got to consider certain things. Again you've got two choices. Unanimous verdict of death and you have the choice [of] life imprisonment for Jimmy Robertson, [who] would spend life in prison without any possibility of parole. You can tell by the prison record this is a difficult place to be. It's not like a country club."

Hancock explained the law about a life sentence without parole; that it truly means life, that no good time or educational pursuits while in prison would lessen the time.

"Jimmy would die in prison," he said. "When I look at the death penalty, I try to look at it in a manner of hope. That when we lose all focus and all faith in any character, any person, and we determine there would be no redeeming value, then we say let's kill him. We lose our hope and our faith that something's going to be better, something's going to happen."

He reviewed the mitigating circumstances and how it applied to James Robertson: He had no prior violent convictions. He had mental illness. He was relatively young.

"Please do not think that in any way I don't have the greatest respect for the lives of Terry and Earl Robertson. You must look, and you must think, and that question comes up. Why? Why? The brutality of this. You can either believe Dr. Pincus or not."

The defense talked about Pincus being paid, but Hancock pointed out that the prosecution's experts and all law enforcement officers were paid as well. Hancock also said Robertson was not a diabolical, conniving criminal. The fact he left a note and then went right where the police could find him proves it.

"What in the world? A person with this much intelligence? What kind of person, in what state of mind, would brutally murder his parents and driving up the road with his cohort say his brother's going to be proud? 'I'm going to tell him about it.' The same brother that at some point in time had planned with him to kill the mama and daddy. What in the world? You have two people and that kid's in jail now. I say 'kid,' he's a young man. Same circumstances, raised in the same household, in the same environment, with the same genetic gene pool, with the same influences, with the same mental diseases as Jimmy and his mama.

"Jimmy didn't look up one day and say, 'I'm going to be a bad kid.'"

He didn't choose to be bipolar and he didn't choose to have ADD, Hancock said.

"He did everything that those diseases tell you to do," Hancock said.

James Robertson went to the state hospital and experts said it was more likely that a person with bipolar disorder would not continue their treatment program, would stop taking medication.

"There were hundreds and hundreds and hundreds of Ritalin tablets in that home ordered from a mail order house; hundreds in that home with the knowledge of those people that were caring for these people that there was abuse taking place. We're not shifting the blame. The blame rests right here," he said, pointing at Robertson. "We're telling what happened.

"I'm not sure any of us could survive the scrutiny of what goes on behind closed doors, but hopefully we will never be the victim; we will never be involved in a murder."

All of Terry Robertson's medical records—not just those read in court—were in evidence and available for review during their deliberations, he said.

Hancock reminded the jurors of the family friends who asked for mercy on Robertson's behalf. The Reverend William Pender, the family's minister, who was in the courtroom, was one, as were people who had known the Robertsons for a long time.

Hancock, standing at the edge of the jury box, looked down for a long moment.

"You have two choices," he said, pausing. "Death, life imprisonment without possibility of parole with no work credits, no early release. You heard other people. Buzzy said he's intelligent, he can contribute to this life in some way, but he will contribute to this life if you give him the chance behind bars until they roll him out to a pauper's grave. He will never see the light of day.

"I ask you do not lose your hope because somewhere there's hope. You can't determine the future. I can't, either. You just have to look at the crime, look at the mitigating circumstances that have been presented to you. Look at the entirety of the experience that we have gone through today and you add your life's experiences, and if you find that anything mitigates this horrible crime, give Jimmy the chance under this controlled environment that Dr. McKee said he was on this medicine doing everything he should. You've got the records from the Corrections Department of South Carolina. If you find any mitigation, if you find it in your heart, if you haven't lost hope, give Jimmy that chance."

James Robertson came from behind the defense table and stood in the middle of the room, facing the jury, his hands in the pockets of his gray slacks. It was the first time the jury had heard his voice.

"In no way could the mitigating factors that my attorneys have presented for me on my behalf excuse what happened that evening. I'm sorry for what happened in the early morning hours about sixteen months ago. I'm sorry for my brother, who has lost his parents. I'm sorry for my grandmother, who lost her only son. I'm sorry for the rest of my family. I'm also sorry for all the friends here and all the people in society that feel for them that were friends of theirs.

"I miss my parents. I must live with this every day of my life. What happened that morning remains so vividly in my mind," he said, starting to cry.

"I'll never be able to explain. I'll never know why or how or anything. I know that it happened. And I can't even explain to my attorneys why it happened. I can't even put it into words, why or how or anything."

He looked up at the ceiling. "I realize, although I don't look forward to it—I don't look forward to spending the rest of my life in prison.

"I realize there are consequences of my actions. I realize I must be held accountable for my actions. I ask you to allow me the continued opportunity to help others in prison, others that were less fortunate."

A single tear rolled down his cheek.

"Others who have not had the educational opportunities that I have had. Allow me to reach out to others so that a similar thing like this never happens— never, ever happens to anybody again. I ask that you spend some time in reaching a verdict. I don't believe that there is any more important decision than you're about to make than one regarding my life. My life is in your hands now. I ask that you spend some time with your decision."

Jurors had watched him closely, but not one cried or showed any emotion.

Robertson walked back to his seat and finally, after eleven days in court, lost complete control of his emotions. He cried and rocked furiously back and forth in his seat. He covered his face with a white legal pad and his body shook as his other attorney, Jim Boyd, began speaking to the jury.

"Ladies and gentlemen, I want you to understand one thing. The evidence that we presented in the defense of this case in the penalty phase of this trial can no way be offered as an excuse for Jimmy Robertson," Boyd said. "If there was an excuse, if there was any justification, it would have been presented at the other phase of the trial. There's no excuse. But what we do have, and what we've tried to present to you, is something to try to show how it came to this point.

"You have a decision between two things; you have a decision between the two worst punishments that can be given in our country. You have a choice of giving the ultimate penalty—the death penalty. You have also the choice of giving the next-to-the-worst penalty, and that's life imprisonment.

"And as Mr. Hancock told you, as the judge will tell you, life is exactly what it says, there's no parole, there's no way for him to get out of prison, ever. He will be in prison, if you give him life, for the rest of his life."

Robertson continued to weep as he rocked back and forth.

"But no matter which way you choose, one way or the other, he's gonna leave prison dead," Boyd continued. "Death is the ultimate penalty. It's the penalty that is reserved for the worst crimes. Now, the law in our state, the law of South Carolina, says you not only have to look at the crime, because if you looked at the crime, if you looked at these pictures, if you looked at everything, your natural inclination is to say, 'Whoever did this deserves to die.'

"But the law says that you have to not only look at the crime, you have to look at the person. And when we look at this, when we with the defense looked at this, and we wondered, 'Well, why, how, could this happen? How could a young man end up killing his parents? How could he end up killing his parents in such a brutal manner?' We looked at that and we asked ourselves why and then we try to find an explanation.

"The state has an explanation that's very simple; that's very simple. Well, he wanted the inheritance so he killed his parents for money. Mr. Brackett characterized him as a 'greedy little man.' Well, let's back up a minute; even if that's true, even if that's true, doesn't that go against every human nature? Who has a desire to kill their parents, even for money? It's not natural. Why? You still have to look at why? So we tried to find out why.

"We tried to find out if something was wrong with him. So we got Dr. Pincus, a neurologist at Georgetown University, former chairman of the department at that prestigious university, a neurologist who wrote the questions that certify other neurologists, to examine him. In his opinion, and the state certainly didn't introduce any testimony in rebuttal to the neurologist, he said in his decision, his frontal lobe doesn't work like other people's. It doesn't work like other people's.

"Now, Mr. Hancock explained to you about the frontal lobe; well, if it doesn't work right, he doesn't have that thing that you and I have, that normal people have, that says no. That says no. We looked; we had doctor evidence, the neuropsychologist examined him, and he came up, in his field, with basically the same conclusions, his frontal lobe doesn't work right.

"The state is asking you to sign a document that

will put Jimmy to death. You know, killing, we are taught, should be necessary, and there are times when it is necessary to kill; obviously, if you're defending yourself, you have a right to kill if necessary to protect yourself and your family. In time of war, we ask soldiers to kill. And sometimes, I submit to you, it's justified and necessary to kill people with the death penalty. But where has the state shown you a necessity to kill Jimmy Robertson? He'll be forced to be in prison for the rest of his life. He'll be where he can't snort Ritalin, where he can't take the illegal drugs. He'll be where he has to take his medication. It's not necessary to kill him. It's just not necessary.

"Now, each of you, as jurors, act, because you sign your name to that document. Each of you act as an individual judge on the fate of Jimmy Robertson. The law never requires that anybody sign that document. The law never requires you to give the death penalty. The law is always totally satisfied with a life sentence.

"We've submitted to you certain mitigating factors, and you as an individual juror have the right to assign whatever weight you want to any mitigating factor that's been presented. And you have a right to do that free from any criticism of anybody in this courtroom or any other juror. You, as an individual, have a right to decide for yourself if any one mitigating factor is sufficient to give Jimmy life. And you have a right to do that regardless of the number of aggravating circumstances you find or how bad those aggravating circumstances are.

"You have a right to find your own mitigating factors. There may be factors that we haven't brought you that you can consider. And you have a right to find those for yourself and give that what weight you think is proper. And you can vote for life even if you find no mitigating factors. You can vote for life if you as an individual find it in your own conscience to do so, and you have a right to have whatever vote you cast respected by the court, by the prosecution, by me and by the other jurors. And you have a right for that respect whether you're voting for life or whether you're voting for death, you each have those rights. And you can give life for basically no reason at all. You can give life just as an act of mercy.

"The first murder that was ever committed was Cain killing Abel. And he was given an act of mercy. He was punished, but his life wasn't taken. It was a family murder, like we have here. I want to think about this case, think about the Robertson family. Mr. Pope talked about how much his father means to him. You know, one thing I've thought about, as I've thought about this case, you know, parents always love their children, no matter what. No matter what.

"There's nothing like the love a parent feels for the child," Boyd said as his eyes welled and his face reddened. "And that's an unconditional love. It doesn't matter if the child loves you back. I didn't really understand until I had my son two years ago." Boyd paused for a moment to compose himself.

"I waited till middle age to start having kids," he continued, "and about two years ago, when I looked in my newborn child's eyes, in the hospital, and I know he couldn't see me at that time, but I made him a promise: that I would always love him."

Boyd, crying, said forcefully, "No matter what. No matter what. If he becomes president of the United States someday, I'll be proud of him, and I hope I'm alive to be here. But if it goes the other way, if he becomes a mass murderer or a serial killer, I'll still love him, and I'll be there for him. And if he kills me, I'll still love him.

"Mr. Pope implies that he speaks for Earl and Terry Robertson. I submit to you, he does not. You heard the preacher who did both their funerals come into the courtroom and ask for mercy. This is a woman who cleaned up the bathrooms at the school when her son was being punished. I don't think that's a good idea. It probably wasn't a good idea. But it does show you what she thought of her child.

"If Jimmy Robertson had killed somebody else, they would be sitting right there behind him. And I submit to you that their spirits don't sit behind that table," Boyd said, pointing to the prosecution. "I submit to you [that] the spirits of Earl and Terry Robertson cry out for you, 'Life.'"

After two weeks, the two sides had given all. Now it was time for the six men and six women of the jury to decide. After Judge Hayes explained the law to them and gave other instructions, they retired to the jury room. It was shortly after six o'clock in the evening.

Hayes and Brackett stayed in the courtroom for the sentencing of Meredith Moon. She was escorted in, wearing a short-sleeved polyester cream-colored dress. She had curled her blond hair the night before, sleeping with her wet hair coiled around rolls from toilet paper. More than a dozen family members, including her parents, and friends fell in behind in a semicircle. Moon stood, her head down, tears running down her cheeks. Her mother, also crying, handed her a tissue.

Harry Dest, the public defender for York County

who was representing Moon, said, "Your Honor, over a year ago, I was appointed to represent Meredith Moon. And I can tell you quite candidly, as a public defender for over nine years now, this is a case that is one of the most unusual, as Your Honor is well aware of.

"One of the most perplexing questions that I've always had since the beginning of my representation of Meredith has been, and still is today, how could someone with so much good in them be involved in something so bad? But again, Your Honor, I have come to learn, and I hope understand, the frailty of human nature and how people who are basically good can make some very bad judgments.

"In November of 1997, Meredith Moon, of course, was arrested for these charges. And I would submit to the court that since that day, she has begun a long journey of rehabilitation. She was cooperative with the police when she was arrested in Philadelphia. She gave statements incriminating herself after waiving her right to counsel. She gave statements as to the details of the event while she was still in Philadelphia to Detective Misle of the York County Sheriff's Office.

"Also, Your Honor, she gave statements regarding the details of the crime. As you recall, she was instrumental in allowing the police to retrieve the evidence that was found in Maryland; she directed them to it. She told them where it was. And again, Your Honor, her cooperation has been from the very beginning to tell the truth.

"When I first met with her, I was struck by how kind, courteous and intelligent she was and still is

today. She told me from the very beginning, 'Mr.
Dest, I just want to do what is right.' And I believe in
her heart she has wanted to do what was right since
the beginning of this case. Again she met with prosecutors; I met with Mr. Pope and Mr. Brackett on
several occasions, on many occasions, while negoti-
ating this case, and I will say for the record that the
solicitor's office has been nothing but fair and open
to us in this matter, while also by not compromising
their duties as prosecutors in this circuit. And for
that we are very grateful.

"They have a job to do, and we also have a job to
do, but we believe both sides have tried to deal with
each other fairly, and that's why we negotiated this
plea agreement. Ms. Moon met with solicitors on
many occasions to discuss the facts of this case. She
also testified in this case, a double-homicide death
penalty case, and I believe that her testimony was
critical and crucial to the prosecution's case.

"And of course the jury has found Mr. Robertson
guilty of two counts of murder, and now is weighing
in their minds whether or not he should receive a
death sentence for his actions.

"Again, I have come to know the Meredith Moon
that is so different than the one of November 1997,
and I will say to the court that every single person in
this room, standing behind her, family and friends,
are here to tell the court, either through letters or
themselves, tell the court that she is someone who
has so much potential. I have come to learn also in
discussions with her, and Dr. Morgan, who you'll
hear from in a few moments, her life has not been
easy.

"Like any young girl who comes from a divorced

situation, she's had struggles with her weight, which of course the court realizes that over a year and a half ago she was two hundred seventy-five pounds, subject of ridicule because of her weight, nicknames given to her because of her weight, created an incredible self-esteem problem. Unfortunately in our society, sometimes we weigh people's value by the way they look rather than the way they are.

"What I know about Meredith in talking to her family, friends and teachers is that she is such a kind person, despite her self-esteem problems, and problems of trying to be accepted into the world and wanting people to like her, she is intelligent and sensitive and always has a kind word. In fact, what I have come to understand in talking to her and Dr. Morgan is that because she is looking for acceptance and looking for people to like her, it made her susceptible to a person such as Jimmy Robertson.

"Her relationship to Jimmy Robertson began in 1995. I believe she will tell you that was the downfall. She began experimenting with alcohol consumption, dabbling in drugs, crack cocaine, marijuana and of course Ritalin as His Honor has heard. But prior to that, in school she was an excellent student, always was in gifted classes. She went to Northwestern High School; she came here at the age of twelve years old; she tried to fit in; she went to Northwestern High School; she was in the Air Force ROTC program for three years, and again she was a gifted student. She scored 1300 on the SATs and had plans of going to college.

"But when she met Jimmy Robertson, that all went downhill. Because of her need to be accepted and her need to feel important, I believe, and I believe the evidence has shown in this case that Jimmy Robertson is a predator. He could control her, tell her what to do, how to do it, and he was the one who dominated her.

"One thing that did not come out in the trial, which I want to say here so that the court has a firm understanding of what type of person he is, a month before the murders, Jimmy Robertson raped my client after she had consumed some alcohol; he raped her, and then after that, she still felt the need to be with him."

Moon, still crying, continued to look down.

"I am not a psychiatrist, but I believe Dr. Morgan will comment in a few moments about that relationship. I believe the defense counsel even presented an expert witness here in this courtroom this week, Dr. Cascio, a social worker, who said, according to Jimmy Robertson, that he could control Meredith and could tell her what to do and that's the defense's own witness. And that reaffirms everything that we have come to understand about this relationship."

Harold Morgan, a forensic psychiatrist who taught at the University of South Carolina, told Hayes, "It's clear she is a very bright young woman has always been in gifted classes. But she's also very sensitive, very emotionally dependent. I think that gets back to some of the early factors in her life. Her parents divorced when she was in the sixth or seventh grade. She lived with her father for the most part after the breakup of the family. Her father had a heart attack. She felt very responsible for him. Early loss with the breakup of the family; with the mother leaving the family, she felt the mother didn't care for her. She felt abandoned and rejected; then her father getting sick, she's afraid he's going to be leaving her. So she's basically sort of sensitized to the idea of abandonment and rejection. That early loss and fear of loss has made her more sensitive to the idea of losing people and having a place to fit in, being accepted.

"Another thing is the lack of a healthy mother figure in the family has prevented her from developing a good clear concept of herself as a healthy mature young woman, and all of that has led to her being very insecure. Although she's bright intellectually, she's very naive in a sense and very insecure on the emotional side of her personality. Her way of compensating for that was to try to fill that void by eating and of course that created more problems. It was a way to insulate her from pain, but she encountered even more rejection by the taunting and whatnot from her peers."

Eventually she found marijuana would relieve anxiety, Morgan said. And the drug world put her in touch with Robertson.

"He seemed to accept her, liked her, and she felt it was a comfortable kind of relationship just to be accepted," Morgan said. "She became enamored of him in that process, though partly because of her neediness."

Morgan said Moon feared Robertson would reject her and therefore never asserted herself or her own needs. He raped her while she was passed out from drinking too much alcohol. Moon never said no to Robertson.

Morgan testified Moon did not have a personality disorder or mental illness, but she did have anxiety and depression. She was not violent, but remained insecure.

"She has the potential to do something with her life," Morgan said.

Teresa Savage, the mother of Moon's best friend, Erin, drove for three and a half hours to speak on Moon's behalf. She considered Moon a member of the family and, in fact, Meredith called her "Mom Savage" and her husband, "Dad Savage." She yearned for a two-parent household.

"I saw Meredith as a girl who respected her elders," Teresa Savage said. "Kind, considerate. Very much wanted to be needed and to have a family life with a mom and dad at home."

Savage said she saw how manipulative Robertson was when he tried to date her daughter. He called relentlessly, rode by their house. Her husband installed caller identification on the phone to see who was calling. When he called one day, Erin's father told Robertson not to call again. After that, he had his brother call on his behalf, every day.

"Meredith's only mistake was she thought she had found someone who loved her," Teresa Savage said.

Also testifying on Moon's behalf was Sergeant Larry Williams, her ROTC teacher at Northwestern High. He called it a "nightmare" to be standing in court that day. He had taught at lot of students in seven years at Northwestern and had thought a few might have ended up where Moon was.

"Ms. Moon is never someone I thought would do this," he said.

She had been promoted to cadet officer material and in leadership roles showed understanding and courtesy to her subordinates. She had much to give.

As each man and woman came to the front of the crowd to talk about her, Moon cried silently. She did not look at them, but kept her head down, her hands clasped in front of her except to wipe her eyes.

Erin Savage told Hayes she had spent the last year and a half defending Meredith to other people who said mean things about her based on what they read in paper.

"I was proud that I was her friend," Savage said. "Best person I know." Erin Savage remembered going with Moon to a farm that had calves. She kissed them and had pictures of herself taken with them.

"I'd think lunch and she'd think precious creatures of God."

Once she was imprisoned, Moon feared her dog, Flip, would think she had abandoned him.

In high school, the ROTC class volunteered to work in the local soup kitchen. "Most of us did it for credit," Savage said. "Meredith really wanted to be there. She was heartbroken when she saw a janitor from our school come in. Give us back Meredith. The world's a better place with her in it and we want her back in our arms."

Valerie Moon, a cousin who looked like a shorter version of Moon, told the judge they had similarities beyond physical. She knew her cousin's character as well as she knew her own. Her cousin's problems stemmed from control and abuse by Robertson.

Crying audibly, Valerie Moon said, "She deserves the mercy of this court. If Robertson had not come into her life, she'd be living with me and going to North Georgia College."

That was what they had planned, what they had dreamed of.

Moon's father, Douglas, sobbed and told about a

time a few years before when they had money problems.

"We were down to two hot dog buns and one hot dog," he recalled. "She said, 'Daddy, you eat it; I don't think I'm hungry.'"

His daughter took care of him through two heart attacks, he told the judge and apologized for crying.

"I wasn't going to cry, Your Honor," Douglas Moon said. "I've cried enough over the last fifteen months to fill this courtroom."

Summing up the forty-five-minute proceeding, Dest said Moon had great potential.

"I believe she can do a lot with her life and I think today is about the future, not the past. She stands before you acknowledging her guilt and is willing to take responsibility for it. Justice demands punishment, but, Your Honor, there is another side of justice in every case. The side of justice that can be tempered with mercy, the side of justice that can give one the hope of redemption, the side of justice that can give one the opportunity to rehabilitate themselves and be a productive citizen."

He said three lives had been destroyed for sure: Earl's, Terry's and James Robertson's.

"The only question is: is Meredith Moon's life destroyed?"

He explained he was asking for an opportunity at redemption.

"I am respectfully requesting you a ten-year sentence for armed robbery to be followed by a consecutive sentence of accessory after the fact, ten years. In my view, that type of sentence would give her a chance at redemption."

Meredith Moon said simply, "Your Honor, for the

past sixteen months, I've had time to think about the judgment calls I've made and the seriousness of them. I am so truly sorry to the Robertson family, my own family and the community. I'm not a bad person. I've just made bad mistakes; you will never realize how truly sorry I am. That's all."

Kevin Brackett, the assistant prosecutor, said, "On behalf of the victims, I ask for mercy as well."

Hayes quickly granted their wish. Moon would be confined to a state penitentiary for ten years for armed robbery, followed by ten years for each of the charges of accessory after the fact. Hayes also credited her with the time she had served in jail since November 27, 1997, almost sixteen months.

Moon knew Robertson had introduced her to evil. She knew that he did not truly care for her, but there remained a tie or some feelings hard to express. It led her, dressed sharply in her cream-colored dress, one hundred pounds thinner, her hair curled, to stand in front of his holding cell as he waited for the jury to decide whether he would live or die. She didn't speak to him or him to her. She just wanted him to see what he was missing.

The jury took three hours and forty minutes to decide Robertson's fate. They sent a note to the judge, and the parties were called back to courtroom 1. It was 9:30 in the evening of the March 26, 1999. James Robertson, twenty-five years old, who should have been in the first years of an engineering career, who should have been married and starting a family, sat down to learn whether he would live or die. He was alone: his mother and father dead, now almost sixteen months to the day, his brother in a cell in another part of the building.

The jury had found five of the ten aggravating circumstances that allowed a death penalty to be imposed in South Carolina. They needed only one. They found that the murders were committed during the commission of an armed robbery and during larceny with a deadly weapon, that physical torture occurred, that he did it for money and that two people were murdered.

The jury said Robertson should die for killing his father.

The same legal terms were spoken about the charge of killing his mother, and again he was sentenced to die.

Robertson looked at the ceiling and rocked wildly in his chair, back and forth. He clasped his hands beneath his chin and placed them on his mouth, his lips quivering. As the verdict was rendered in the death of his mother, he put his fingers in his ears, a vain attempt to push reality from his mind. Robertson dropped his head into his hands and sobbed, a tissue in his hands. His body was racked in anguish. Yet when he put his face up, in view, there were no visible tears.

Linda Weaver, Terry's longtime friend, told the news media after the sentencing that the two weeks of the trial were the longest of her life. But there was relief in the sentence.

"For once in his life, he's going to have to pay for what he's done," she said.

Misle escorted Robertson outside when officers came to the York County Jail that night to take Robertson to Kirkland Correctional Institution in Columbia, South Carolina, where he would be evaluated before being sent to death row. Justice had been served, Misle thought, the angry young man was going where he belonged. Misle asked Robertson if he wanted the five cents that was in his pocket when he was booked sixteen months earlier. Robertson said he didn't. Misle threw a nickel in the floorboard of the patrol car. It was a gesture of contempt.

Chip Robertson heard the news that night in a phone call he made collect to a friend. Chip Robertson had been in York County Jail for about three months awaiting disposition of charges unrelated—yet completely related—to the murders of his parents. After their deaths, he dropped out of college, abused drugs and was arrested for check forgery and distribution of cocaine and Xanax.

The arrest came outside a Holiday Inn in Rock Hill on the day before New Year's Eve, 1998. He had 8.7 grams of cocaine and six tablets and eleven pieces of the prescription tranquilizer. He also was charged with giving two checks—one for $350 and another for $500—to someone to cash. His plan was to report the checks stolen from the account managed by the bank that was acting as executor of his parents' estates and then split the money with the man who cashed them, police said.

He stayed in jail, unable to make the $70,000 bond, and even though he was imprisoned in the same facility as his brother for three months, he never saw him or talked with him.

In May 1999, two months after his brother was sent to death row, Chip Robertson pleaded guilty. His lawyer, Mike Gillen of Rock Hill, told Judge Thomas Cooper his client had "gone downhill in a hurry." If he hadn't been arrested, he'd have killed himself with drugs, and a return to drug use would likely kill him as well.

"I was looking at death," said Chip Robertson, who had gained forty pounds in jail. "I really think I was rescued. This has been a blessing for me. I just want you to know I won't get in any more trouble."

Cooper sentenced him to five years' probation and three months at Hazelden, the renowned drug rehabilitation program in Minnesota. The $13,000 cost of the program and $185 a day for room and board—at least $16,650 for the ninety days the court required he be there—would be paid by his parents' estates.

At the time Chip Robertson was sentenced, police said they were still looking for evidence that he was in some way involved in the murders. By 2003, though, he had not been charged.

Gillen acknowledged Chip Robertson had talked about killing his parents but had nothing to do with the murders.

"To have his brother actually do it—I think his grief is compounded," the lawyer said. "Saying something and doing something are drastically different things."

James Robertson's trial had taken eleven days in the courtroom, from the start of jury selection on a Monday morning to the sentencing on the Friday of the next week. It cost the people of York County about $150,000. His lawyers earned about $20,000 a piece. Assorted experts took in fees for evaluations and testimony. The state of South Carolina spends about $17,000 a year to keep Robertson on death row.

But what can't be calculated is the toll on the lives of those left behind: the friends, who were forever changed when the intimate details of the Robertsons' lives became dinner conversation for people they had never met; the jurors, who saw pictures of hacked and bludgeoned bodies far worse than anything that can be imagined; Chip Robertson, who despite his new-found wealth will go through life without a compass; and then James Robertson himself, locked in a much more chilling place than South Carolina's death row—his own self-absorbed, egomaniacal, ruthless mind.

During a psychological evaluation performed for his defense, Robertson complained to a social worker that some of his parents' friends never visited him in jail.

"Family friends didn't think of me," he said. "I lost two parents."

Part 4
The Aftermath

Chapter 24

South Carolina's death row is a relatively small place—a one-story brick building beside the much larger Lieber Correctional Institution near Ridgeville, a little town about an hour west of the historic port city of Charleston. It is way out in the country and a serenely quiet place, more like a public library than a prison. The men whisper to each other or to the counselors or guards, who are the only people allowed on the cell block. Some rarely speak. One, a young man who killed two children in an elementary-school cafeteria, passes his days curled up in a fetal position on his bunk. Prison administrators say death row inmates are the best behaved of all prisoners.

In 1999, when James Robertson arrived on the row, about seventy men were confined to the six-by-eight-foot cells, where they spend twenty-three hours out of every day. They get one hour out of each day to take showers or to mingle six at a time in outdoor recreation pens that look like dog runs. Inmates whose executions are imminent are segregated during recreation.

Robertson stood apart from the other inmates, just as he stood apart from the students in his schools or the members of his church youth group.

By far, he was the best educated and most intelligent of those condemned to death row. Some of the men there barely had a high-school education. Only a handful had ever been to college.

One of his best friends, he said, was Michael Passaro, who set his daughter on fire in her car seat outside his estranged wife's condominium in Myrtle Beach. Passaro dropped all his appeals and chose to be executed in 2002 after barely a year on the row. He was the first in the state to be executed without any appeals.

For a time, Robertson thought he would drop his appeals as well. Robertson asked the South Carolina Supreme Court to order the state to execute him immediately. He reasoned that would save him at least eight years of tedium. But he elected to drop that request and then petitioned the court to be his own lawyer. In a hearing before Judge Hayes, the same judge who presided over Robertson's trial, Robertson said he had asked his attorneys for two years to drop his appeals.

"Attorneys said they would help do that and walked out and asked the supreme court to do the opposite," Robertson told the judge. He said his relationship with his appeals lawyer, Joseph Savitz, was adversarial, not smooth.

He testified he was taking Prozac, Lithium and Vistaril to control bipolar illness.

Savitz told the *Rock Hill Herald* after Robertson's hearing that Robertson was trying to manipulate the system and that he could have won the case on appeal.

"Mr. Robertson is not as smart as he thinks he is,"

Savitz told the newspaper. "The crimes he is charged with were not the crimes of an intelligent man."

Hayes agreed in late October 2002 to let Robertson represent himself.

"While he does have mental health issues, Robertson is fully capable and competent to act knowingly and intelligently on his own behalf," Hayes wrote.

It was classic Robertson, thinking he could defend himself, that he could navigate the tricky back roads of criminal law better than a lawyer. In late 2002, Robertson said he wasn't sure what he would do once he received permission to represent himself. He might play the system for a time, and when he decides he's ready to die, he'll drop his appeals. Or he might just tie the system up for years. He wanted to be in control.

On death row, cell-to-cell communication is difficult. The walls are concrete, the door metal with a window and a small opening for food to be passed through. The solitude is perhaps toughest on someone like Robertson, who enjoys what he considers to be the adoration or at least attention of others. The restriction on books—no more than ten at a time—is difficult for the voracious reader. Robertson can have only a bound volume of pictures or ten loose pictures. He wears the forest green jumpsuit of death row whenever he is outside his cell.

He has a bunk bed and a metal desk. Two thin rectangular windows bring in the only light. Robertson spends a great deal of time writing to people in the outside world. He fills pages of legal-pad paper or types missives, usually in all capital letters. He has written to schoolchildren and newspaper reporters. He wrote to Meredith Moon and blamed her for his predicament. He has also offered her legal advice. He advised that one avenue she might want to pursue is to question her lawyer's handling of the case, to assert he took what Robertson called the "quick fix." Robertson also said mistakes were made, but he wouldn't tell her what they were. If he did, it would free them both, he said, a "morally corrupt" position. He believes they should both be punished for what they did.

He did provide her with hints. The indictments were false, he said, based on lies.

"Can you honestly say to me that you know what happened upstairs that night? Can you tell me for sure that even my parents were in the house? Can you say that all the blood didn't come from killing the dog or the cat? I know the answer—answer it yourself."

He said if he had caught the mistakes before the trial he'd have turned it into a "full-fledged circus."

In four years on death row, Robertson had not changed. He still wanted to feel like he was calling the shots. He still wanted to feel like the big man, the center of attention, the celebrity. He told her he was going to arrange to have his typewriter auctioned on eBay after he was executed.

In early 2003, Meredith Moon celebrated her twenty-fourth birthday at Leath Correctional Institution in Greenwood, South Carolina. Leath, a spotless and relatively new facility, houses about a thousand women. Moon tends to pal around with other women who have long sentences for violent crimes. That is the nature of prison. She said one of her closest friends was Susan Smith, who was sent to Leath from Women's Correctional Institution in 2001 after it became known she and a guard had had sex.

Moon's parents visit almost every other week, sitting at a table for four in the large visitation room, with dozens of other women, some of whom are passing the few hours a month they can spend with their children. Moon's parents provide her with enough money to ease the burdens of prison. She buys makeup and all manner of food products from the canteen to cook innovative meals in a microwave for her friends. She has managed to keep off the weight she lost after her arrest.

Moon gives presentations to teens in trouble, laying out her story with the hope it will keep another young person out of prison. She has also been a part of a group that provides spiritual-based therapy. It has helped her come to terms with her past and her family life and to understand why she would become so dependent on someone like James Robertson.

Moon sometimes cries when she thinks of Terry and Earl Robertson and her role in their deaths. If anything, time has made her feel more guilt. She still wonders why she did not run for help, why she sat there stupidly on a couch in Robertson's bedroom and listened to Terry Robertson scream, "No, Jimmy." She hears it still. She says the first thing she wants to do when she gets out of prison is go to their gravesite in Milledgeville, Georgia, and put flowers on their graves. She knows it is an empty gesture, but it is all she can do. Nothing can make up for what was taken from Earl and Terry and the people who loved them. She will be eligible for parole in 2006.

Robertson writes to her on occasion, sometimes including explicit descriptions of sex acts. He told her in one letter he considers prison a long-awaited vacation and in another a dehumanizing existence where people start believing they are bad people, rather than human beings who did a bad thing.

He considers the death penalty inhumane, retribution, not punishment and certainly not something that would keep murders from taking place. He complained that he was being judged by his ten worst minutes.

He keeps in touch with his brother, who completed his time at Hazelden Clinic in Minnesota and in 2003 was preparing to graduate from college. James Robertson told Moon his brother intended to spend six weeks studying in the Czech Republic in 2000 and that they had made up. They were not friends, he said, but brothers.

Probate court records show Chip Robertson inherited the Rock Hill and Grand Rapids houses, his mother's jewelry and his father's baseball cards. He sold his father's van and his mother's Cadillac. He sold the house on Westminster in 2000 to a couple for $125,000, far less than its appraised value. Bicycles and children's toys once again can be seen scattered about the driveway and the yard.

Taxes took more than $200,000 from the estate and extraneous bills reaped thousands more. By the time the wills were probated in the fall of 2001, Chip Robertson had received checks from the estate in the amount of $665,000. The cases are closed, all but forgotten in a cardboard filing box inside a building in downtown York, South Carolina, that once housed a Belk department store.

In 2003, Judge Hayes was still on the bench; Jim Boyd and Bill Hancock were still practicing criminal law in Rock Hill; Thomas Pope was still solicitor of York and Union counties. Pope was approached to run for statewide office but declined. He spent several months traveling every other week to California to tape *Power of Attorney,* a syndicated late-night television show similar to *People's Court* but with real-life lawyers. It featured him and several other attorneys, including Marcia Clark and Chris Darden, two of the prosecutors in the O.J. Simpson murder trial, and Gloria Allred, a Los Angeles attorney instrumental in cases involving women's rights. The show was billed as offering an opportunity for everyday folk to have the benefit of representation from high-profile lawyers.

He enjoyed it and for a time wondered if he needed a publicist.

"I'd Southernize mine up some," Pope said. "It was just fun."

His favorite times, though, are those spent with his wife and sons on their farm outside of Rock Hill. In his forties, he consciously doused some of the flames that drove him so hard early in his career.

"I used to run on sheer passion, adrenaline, anger, indignation," he said. "But like a rag that was wrung out, I've evolved. I'm passionate about it, but I contain it."

Television offers kept coming. Among them, a spot on women who kill their children after Andrea Yates was arrested in the murders of her five children in Texas. Like Susan Smith, Yates did not receive the death penalty. The Susan Smith case remains with Pope.

James Robertson wrote to him to say he had seen *Power of Attorney* on death row. In fact, Robertson has written to Pope many times. Once, he complained about Brackett, who in 2003 was serving as second-in-charge of the Sixteenth Circuit Solicitor's Office.

Robertson told Pope that Brackett didn't deserve to shine Pope's shoes. Pope keeps a shoe shine kit underneath his desk to gig Brackett about that comment. Pope was surprised by a Christmas card Robertson sent him the first year he was on death row. James Robertson wished him and "his colleagues" a happy holiday season and offered best wishes to him and his family.

"If you didn't know better, you would have thought it was from a neighbor's kid," Pope said.

In a way, it was.

ABOUT THE AUTHOR

Lyn Riddle is the city editor of the *Greenville News* in Greenville, South Carolina. Her work has also appeared in the *New York Times*, the *Los Angeles Times* and the *Atlanta Constitution*. She lives with her husband and children in Simpsonville, South Carolina.

MORE MUST-READ TRUE CRIME
FROM PINNACLE

HORRIFYING TRUE CRIME
FROM PINNACLE BOOKS